THE ULTIMATE FRESH PASTA AT HOME COOKBOOK

100 incredible recipes for mastering the age-old art of making pasta at home and impressing friends and family

FIONA FONDA

All rights reserved.

Disclaimer

The information contained in this eBook is meant to serve as a comprehensive collection of strategies that the author of this eBook has done research about. Summaries, strategies, tips, and tricks are only recommendations by the author, and reading this eBook will not guarantee that one's results will exactly mirror the author's results. The author of the eBook has made all reasonable efforts to provide current and accurate information for the readers of the eBook. The author and its associates will not be held liable for any unintentional error or omissions that may be found. The material in the eBook may include information by third parties. Third-party materials comprise opinions expressed by their owners. As such, the author of the eBook does not assume responsibility or liability for any third-party material or opinions. Whether because of the progression of the internet, or the unforeseen changes in company policy and editorial submission guidelines, what is stated as fact at the time of this writing may become outdated or inapplicable later.

The eBook is copyright © 2022 with all rights reserved. It is illegal to redistribute, copy, or create derivative work from this eBook whole or in part. No parts of this report may be reproduced or retransmitted in any reproduced or retransmitted in any forms whatsoever without the writing expressed and signed permission from the author.

TABLE OF CONTENTS

TABLE OF CONTENTS 3
INTRODUCTION 7
DOUGH 8
   1.   SEMOLINA DOUGH 9
   2.   DRY DOUGH 11
   3.   BASIC PASTA DOUGH 13
POULTRY PASTA 15
   4.   CHICKEN TETRAZZINI 16
   5.   CRÈME FRAICHE CHICKEN PASTA 19
   6.   PAD THAI 22
   7.   CHICKEN LASAGNA 25
   8.   CURRY CHICKEN PASTA SALAD 27
   9.   ASIAN CHICKEN SALAD 29
   10. DRUNKEN NOODLES 31
   11. CHICKEN SKILLET DISH ITALIAN STYLE 34
   12. CHICKEN AND SHRIMP CARBONARA 36
   13. ROSEMARY PASTA SHELLS SOUP 39
   14. BELL PASTA 42
   15. SMOKED SUNDRIED TOMATO SOUP 45
   16. CHEESY CHICKEN CREAM PASTA 48
   17. CLASSICAL ALFREDO 51
   18. EASY ITALIAN PARMIGIANA 54
   15. CHICKEN FROM MILAN 57
   16. NUTTY CHICKEN PASTA 60
   17. CHICKEN TENDERS AND FARFALLE SALAD 63
   18. CHICKEN ALFREDO LASAGNA 66
   19. CHICKEN TETRAZZINI 69

20.	ANGEL HAIR SHRIMP BAKE	72
21.	CURRY LASAGNA	74
22.	BAKED RIGATONI AND MEATBALLS	77
23.	BAKED PENNE WITH TURKEY MEATBALLS	79

FISH/SEAFOOD PASTA 82

24.	PESTO SHRIMP WITH PASTA	83
25.	MACARONI SEAFOOD SALAD	85
26.	SMOKED SALMON PASTA	87
27.	BAY SCALLOPS WITH SPAGHETTI	89
28.	CRAB SALAD	91
29.	SHRIMP LO MEIN	93
30.	SHRIMP CARBONARA	95
31.	LOBSTER MAC AND CHEESE	98
36.	TUNA PASTA	101
37.	SHRIMP SCAMPI	104
38.	CLASSICAL PENNE PASTA	106
39.	LINGUINE AND CLAM SAUCE	109

MEAT PASTA 111

40.	BOLOGNESE SAUCE	112
41.	BEEF STROGANOFF	115
42.	SAUCY BEEF SKILLET	117
43.	CLASSICAL LASAGNA	120
44.	SAUCY CHEDDAR FUSILLI SALAD	123
45.	PENNE BEEF BAKE	126
46.	CHILI MAC CASSEROLE	128
47.	THREE-CHEESE MEATBALL MOSTACCIOLI	130
48.	BAKED ZITI	133
49.	EASY SPAGHETTI	136
50.	HUNGARIAN GOULASH	138

VEGETABLE PASTA 140

    51. SPINACH LASAGNA 141
    52. PROVOLONE ZITI BAKE 144
    53. RATATOUILLE LASAGNA 146
    54. EGGPLANT CANNELLONI 150
    55. ARTICHOKE SPINACH PASTA SAUCE 153
    56. EGGPLANT MEZZALUNA AND TOMATO CONFIT 155
    57. GROWN-UP TOMATO-PARMESAN PASTA 159
    58. PUMPKIN AND SAGE LASAGNA WITH FONTINA 162
    59. MINTY FETA AND ORZO SALAD 165
    60. FRESH LEMON PASTA 168
    61. TORTELLINI JARRED SALAD 171
    62. ROMANO LINGUINE PASTA SALAD 173
    63. VEGAN RIGATONI BASIL 176
    64. BLT PASTA SALAD 179
    65. NOODLE KUGEL 181
    66. TORTELLINI PESTO SALAD 183
    67. CONFETTI PASTA SALAD 185
    68. CAPRESE PASTA SALAD 187
    69. MOZZARELLA FRITTERS AND SPAGHETTI 189
    70. ONE-POT CREAMED CORN BUCATINI 192
    71. SPINACH AND ARTICHOKE MAC-AND-CHEESE 195
    72. DECADENT SPINACH-STUFFED SHELLS 198
    73. BUTTERNUT AND CHARD PASTA BAKE 200

SAUSAGE PASTA 203

    74. SOUTHWESTERN LASAGNA 204
    75. ROMANO RIGATONI CASSEROLE 206
    76. CHEESY PEPPERONI ROTINI SALAD 209
    77. ROMAN FUN PASTA 211
    78. TORTELLINI CLASSICO 214

- 79. Spanish Lasagna 217
- 80. Ziti with Sausage 220
- 81. Saucy Lasagna 223
- 82. Slow Cooker Lasagna 226
- 83. Penne and Smoked Sausage 228
- 84. Spinach and three-cheese stuffed shells 230
- 85. Classical Lasagna II 233
- 86. Pepperoni Lasagna 237

CLASSIC PASTA 240

- 87. Ramen Noodle Salad 241
- 88. Angel Hair Carbonara 243
- 89. Penne with Vodka Sauce 245
- 90. Penne alla vodka 247
- 91. Lemon basil pasta with brussels sprouts 250
- 92. Crimini Pasta Bake 253
- 93. Sunny Hot Spaghetti 256
- 94. Puttanesca 258
- 95. Parmesan Orzo 261
- 96. Pasta Rustica 264
- 97. Egg noodle in Germany 267
- 98. Italian Noodles with Croutons 269
- 99. Loaded Pasta Shells Lasagna 271
- 100. Scuola di Pasta 273

CONCLUSION 276

INTRODUCTION

The ingredients that are used to make fresh pasta are flour and eggs and optionally salt. This is leads to one of the most puzzling aspects of making homemade pasta. With just two main ingredients you would be forgiven for wondering what all the fuss is about. How can it be difficult? Well, of course it doesn't have to be difficult.

There are simple recipes that if followed carefully with the right amount of liquid and the right type of flour will produce excellent results every time. It's just that there are so many ways in which to vary the recipes to produce desirable results that it is worth just considering the variables at play.

Now the classic Italian flour used for every day pasta is known in Italy and in some other countries as '00' flour. The Italians use a scale of 00 to 04 to indicate the colour of the flours. The colour depends on how much bran and germ have been 'extracted' from the flour. The bran and germ are what gives flour its colour. The '00' therefore has had all the bran and germ removed and so is a very white and smooth flour which of course produces silky-smooth pasta that is ideal for many uses.

Other than in these special cases, gluten is a key component of the pasta making process. When mixed with the fluid and allowed to stand for a while, Gluten forms bonds at the chemical level. This makes the dough stretchy and springy. It holds the dough together and prevents it from crumbling or falling apart. Gluten is the same ingredient that gives bread dough its properties.

DOUGH

1. Semolina Dough

Ingredients

- 2 1/2 cups all-purpose flour, plus more for dusting
- 1 3/4 cups semolina
- 1 1/4 cups water

Directions

a) Combine the flour, semolina, and water in the bowl of a standing mixer fitted with the paddle attachment and mix on low speed until the dough comes together.

b) Turn off the mixer, remove the paddle attachment, and replace it with the dough hook. Scrape down the sides of the bowl and beat the dough with the dough hook on medium speed until it forms a ball, about 5 minutes. Dust a flat work surface with flour.

c) Turn the dough out onto the dusted surface and gently knead it for 20 to 25 minutes, until the ball begins to feel elastic and the surface of the dough feels smooth and silky.

d) Wrap the dough in plastic wrap and refrigerate to rest for at least 45 minutes and up to overnight before sheeting it.

2. Dry Dough

Ingredients

- 1 1/2 cups all-purpose flour, plus more for dusting
- 12 extra-large egg yolks (16 ounces of yolks), whisked together in a medium bowl

Directions

a) Put the flour in the bowl of a standing mixer fitted with the paddle attachment and begin to run the machine at low speed. With the mixer running, add the egg yolks gradually, mixing until the dough comes together. Turn off the mixer and dust a flat work surface with flour.

b) Turn the dough out onto the dusted surface, form it into a ball, and gently knead it for 20 to 25 minutes, until the ball begins to feel elastic and the surface of the dough feels smooth and silky.

c) Wrap the dough in plastic wrap and refrigerate to rest for at least 45 minutes and up to overnight before sheeting it.

3. Basic Pasta Dough

Ingredients

- 2 1/4 cups all-purpose flour, plus more for dusting
- 3 extra-large eggs
- 6 extra-large egg yolks

Directions

a) Put the flour, eggs, and egg yolks in the bowl of a standing mixer fitted with the paddle attachment and mix on low speed until the dough comes together. Turn off the mixer, remove the paddle attachment, and replace it with the dough hook.

b) Scrape down the sides of the bowl and beat the dough with the dough hook on medium speed until it forms a ball, about 5 minutes. Dust a flat work surface with flour.

c) Turn the dough out onto the dusted surface and gently knead it for 20 to 25 minutes, until the ball begins to feel elastic and the surface of the dough feels smooth and silky.

d) Wrap the dough in plastic wrap and refrigerate to rest for at least 45 minutes and up to overnight before sheeting it.

POULTRY PASTA

4. Chicken Tetrazzini

Servings Size: 8

Ingredients
- 8 oz. spaghetti
- 1 Tablespoons olive oil
- 4 shredded chicken breasts
- Salt and pepper to taste
- 1 cup fresh sliced mushrooms
- 1 chopped red bell pepper
- 1 chopped onion
- 4 minced garlic cloves
- $\frac{1}{4}$ cup butter
- 3 Tablespoons flour
- $\frac{1}{2}$ teaspoons thyme
- 1 cup chicken broth
- 1 cup half-and-half
- $\frac{1}{4}$ cup white wine
- $\frac{1}{2}$ teaspoons garlic salt
- $\frac{1}{2}$ teaspoons oregano
- Pepper to taste
- $\frac{1}{2}$ cup shredded Italian cheese mix

Directions
a) Cook the spaghetti in a pot of boiling salted water for 10 minutes.
b) Heat the oil in a large skillet.
c) Brown the bell pepper, mushrooms, onion, and garlic into the skillet and sauté for 5 minutes, until the vegetables are soft and the chicken no longer pink.
d) Melt the butter in a pan and stir in the flour.
e) Keep stirring until a paste is created.

f) Slowly pour in the broth, half-and-half, and wine while continuously stirring.
g) Season the sauce with pepper, oregano, and thyme.
h) Stir in the Italian cheese blend and stir for 5 minutes, until the cheese is melted.
i) Add the browned and vegetables and simmer for 5 minutes.

5. Crème Fraiche Chicken Pasta

Servings Size: 4

Ingredients
- 1 Tablespoons olive oil
- 6 chicken fillets
- ¼ cup white wine
- ¼ cup chicken broth
- Salt and pepper to taste
- 8 oz. bow tie pasta
- 2 Tablespoons chopped shallots
- 3 minced garlic cloves
- 1 cup sliced mushrooms
- 2 cups crème fraiche
- 1/3 cup grated Parmesan cheese
- 2 Tablespoons chopped parsley

Directions
a) Heat the oil in a large skillet.
b) Brown the chicken for 5 minutes.
c) Pour in the wine and broth and season with salt and pepper.
d) Simmer for 20 minutes.
e) While the chicken is simmering, cook the pasta in a pot of salted water for 10 minutes and drain. Set aside.
f) Use a tong to transfer the chicken to a platter and cube the chicken.
g) Add the onion, garlic, and mushrooms to the skillet and sauté for 5 minutes.
h) Return the cubed chicken to the skillet and stir in the crème fraiche.
i) Simmer for 5 minutes.

j) Place the pasta in a serving bowl and pour the sauce over the pasta.
k) Top with parmesan cheese and chopped parsley.

6. Pad Thai

Servings Size: 6

Ingredients
- 12 oz., rice noodles
- 2 Tablespoons peanut oil
- ½ cups cubed chicken
- 3 minced garlic cloves
- 3 chopped scallions
- 1 Tablespoons olive oil
- 4 eggs
- 2 teaspoons sweet chili sauce
- 1 Tablespoons white wine vinegar
- 2 Tablespoons fish sauce
- 1 teaspoon, lime juice
- 1 Tablespoons peanut sauce
- 2 Tablespoons, sugar
- ¼ cup crushed peanuts

Directions
a) Soak the rice noodles in a bowl of water for 5 minutes. Drain and set aside.
b) Heat the peanut oil in a large skillet.
c) Brown the garlic, scallions, and chicken for 5 minutes.
d) Transfer the chicken to a plate and set aside.
e) Heat the olive oil in the same skillet and crack the eggs into the skillet.
f) Scramble the eggs until they are firm, about 5 minutes.
g) Stir in the chili sauce, white wine vinegar, fish sauce, lime juice, peanut sauce, and sugar.
h) Stir well.
i) Return the chicken to the skillet and cook for 3 minutes.

j) Transfer the noodles into the skillet and toss well.
k) Top with the crushed peanuts.

7. Chicken Lasagna

Servings Size: 6

Ingredients
- 6 uncooked lasagna noodles, boiled
- 1 cup shredded cooked chicken
- 1 Tablespoons olive oil
- ½ lb. chopped mushrooms
- 1 chopped red bell pepper
- 1 chopped small onion
- 3 minced garlic cloves
- ¼ cup chicken broth
- 8 oz., cream cheese
- ½ teaspoons oregano
- Salt and pepper to taste
- 2 cups shredded mozzarella cheese
- 3 cups tomato sauce

Directions

a) Preheat the oven to 350 degrees F.
b) Heat the olive oil in a skillet and sauté the mushrooms, bell pepper, onion, and garlic for 5 minutes.
c) Combine the shredded chicken, broth, cream cheese, mushrooms, bell pepper, onion, garlic, and oregano in a bowl.
d) Stir in 1 cup mozzarella cheese and season with salt and pepper.
e) Pour 1 cup of tomato sauce into a 9x13 baking dish.
f) Create three layers of lasagna noodles, chicken mixture, and tomato sauce.
g) Top with the remaining cup of shredded mozzarella cheese.
h) Bake for 45 minutes.

8. Curry Chicken Pasta Salad

Servings Size: 6

Ingredients
- 8 oz. pasta shells
- 1 cup mayonnaise
- 1 cup sour cream
- 3 cups cubed cooked chicken
- $\frac{1}{2}$ cup chopped walnuts
- $\frac{1}{2}$ cup raisins
- 2 teaspoons curry powder
- Salt and pepper to taste
- 3 chopped scallions

Directions
a) Cook the pasta in a pot of salted boiling water for 10 minutes. Drain and let cool.
b) Combine the mayonnaise, sour cream, chicken, walnuts, raisins, curry powder, salt, pepper, and scallions in a bowl.
c) Stir in the pasta.
d) Refrigerate the pasta for 3 hours.

9. Asian Chicken Salad

Servings Size: 4

Ingredients
- 2 Tablespoons brown sugar
- 1 Tablespoons soy sauce
- 2 Tablespoons sesame oil
- 3 Tablespoons rice vinegar
- 1 head chopped napa lettuce
- 1 ½ cups shredded chicken meat
- 4 chopped scallions
- 1 peeled and grated carrot
- 1 cup sugar snap peas
- ¼ cup mandarin orange slices
- 2 teaspoons toasted sesame seeds
- 3 Tablespoons slivered almonds
- 8 oz. canned fried noodles

Directions
a) Combine the brown sugar, soy sauce, sesame oil, and rice vinegar and pour in a container.
b) Let sit for 30 minutes
c) Combine the napa lettuce, chicken, scallions, carrot, snap peas, and orange slices in a large bowl.
d) Toss with the salad dressing.
e) Top with the sesame seeds, slivered almonds, and canned fried noodles.

10.   Drunken Noodles

Servings Size: 6

Ingredients
- ¼ cup rice vinegar
- 2 Tablespoons fish sauce
- Juice of half a lemon
- 1 Tablespoons brown sugar
- 1 Tablespoons sriracha sauce
- ¾ cup chopped chicken meat
- 16 oz. wide rice noodles – cooked according to package instructions
- ¼ cup canola oil
- 4 minced garlic cloves
- 1 small, diced onion
- ½ cup oyster sauce
- 2 Tablespoons soy sauce
- 3 peeled and grated carrots
- 1 diced tomato
- 1 cup sliced mushrooms
- ½ baby corn
- 3 Tablespoons chopped scallions
- 1 cup chopped cilantro

Directions
a) Combine the rice vinegar, fish sauce, lemon juice, brown sugar, and sriracha sauce in a bowl.
b) Add the chicken and coat well.
c) Marinade the chicken for 1 hour.
d) Heat the canola oil in a skillet
e) Sauté the garlic and onion for 5 minutes.
f) Add the chicken with the marinade and stir well.

g) Simmer for 10 minutes.
h) Stir in the remaining ingredients and keep stirring for 5 minutes.

11.   Chicken Skillet Dish Italian Style

Servings Size: 4

Ingredients
- 1 Tablespoons olive oil
- 1 ½ cups cubed chicken
- 4 minced garlic cloves
- 1 chopped onion
- 1 chopped green bell pepper
- 1 chopped red bell pepper
- ½ cup red wine
- 1 (28 oz.) can diced tomato with juices
- ½ cup chicken broth
- 1 teaspoons Italian seasoning or to taste
- 8 oz. small shell pasta
- 6 oz. chopped spinach
- 1 cup grated parmesan cheese
- 2 teaspoons chopped basil

Directions
a) Heat the olive oil in a large skillet and brown the chicken for 5 minutes.
b) Add the garlic, onion, and peppers and sauté for 5 more minutes.
c) Stir in the wine, tomatoes with juices, the broth, and Italian seasoning.
d) Bring the liquid to a boil and add the pasta to the skillet.
e) Cook the pasta on medium heat for 10 minutes, until they are done.
f) Add the spinach and parmesan cheese and simmer for 5 more minutes.
g) Serve topped with chopped basil.

12.   Chicken and Shrimp Carbonara

Servings Size: 6

Ingredients
- ¼ cup olive oil, divided
- 1 lb. chicken cubes
- 4 Tablespoons minced garlic, divided
- 1 teaspoons thyme
- 1 teaspoons oregano
- 1 teaspoons basil
- 1 lb. peeled and deveined shrimp
- 16 oz. linguine
- 6 sliced diced bacon
- Salt and pepper to taste
- 1 chopped onion
- 1 cup sliced mushrooms
- 1 chopped red bell pepper
- 2 cup heavy cream
- 1 cup milk
- 1 ½ cups grated Parmesan cheese
- 2 egg yolks
- 1 cup white wine.

Directions
a) Heat 2 Tablespoons olive in a large pan.
b) Sauté half the garlic and season with thyme, oregano, and basil.
c) Stir in the chicken and cook on low for 10 minutes.
d) Place the chicken on a platter and set aside.
e) Using the same pan, heat 2 Tablespoons olive oil and sauté the remaining garlic for 2 minutes.
f) Stir in the shrimp and cook on low for 6 minutes.

g) Transfer the shrimp with the chicken.
h) Cook the linguine in a pot of salted water for 12 minutes.
i) Again, using the same pan, fry the bacon until done, about 5 minutes.
j) Drain the bacon on a paper towel and crumble. Set aside.
k) Sauté the onion, bell pepper, and mushroom in the pan with the bacon fat for 5 minutes.
l) Combine the heavy cream, milk, parmesan cheese, egg yolks, salt, and pepper in a bowl.
m) Add the wine to the onion, pepper, and mushroom in the pan and bring to a boil.
n) Cook on low for 5 minutes.
o) Stir in the heavy cream mixture and simmer for 5 minutes.
p) Return the shrimp and chicken to the pan and coat with the sauce.
q) Serve the shrimp and chicken with the pasta.

13.   Rosemary Pasta Shells Soup

SERVES 4

Ingredients

- 2 teaspoons olive oil
- 1/2 C. whole wheat pasta shells or 1/2 C. shell
- 1 garlic clove, finely minced
- pasta
- 1 shallot, finely diced
- 1 teaspoons rosemary
- 3 -4 C. fat-free chicken broth or 3 -4 C.
- 3 C. Baby Spinach, cleaned and trimmed
- vegetable stock
- 1/8 teaspoons black pepper
- 1 (14 1/2 oz.) can diced tomatoes
- 1 dash crushed red pepper flakes
- 1 (14 1/2 oz.) can of white beans (cannellini or other)

Directions

a) Place a large saucepan on medium heat. Heat the oil in it. Add the garlic and shallot then cook them for 4 min.

b) Stir in the broth, tomatoes, beans, and rosemary, black and red pepper. Cook them until they start boiling. Stir in the pasta and simmer the soup for 12 min.

c) Stir in the spinach and simmer the soup until it wilts. Serve the soup warm.

d) Enjoy.

14.   Bell pasta

SERVES 8

Ingredients

- 1 Tablespoons olive oil
- 1 1/2 C. kidney beans, cooked
- 1 onion, chopped
- 2 teaspoons chopped fresh thyme
- 2 cloves garlic, minced
- 1/2 C. chopped spinach
- 1 red bell pepper, chopped
- 1 C. seashell pasta
- 3 C. low fat, low chicken broth
- ground black pepper to taste
- 1 C. canned whole tomatoes, chopped

Directions

a) Place a large pot on medium heat. Heat the oil in it. Add the onion and garlic then cook them for 5 min. Stir in the bell pepper and cook them for 3 min.

b) Stir in the broth, tomatoes, and beans. Cook them until they start boiling. Lower the heat and simmer the soup for 20 min.

c) Add the thyme, spinach, and pasta. Cook the soup for 5 min. Adjust the seasoning of the soup. Serve it warm.

d) Enjoy.

15. Smoked Sundried Tomato Soup

SERVES 8

Ingredients

- 2 slices turkey bacon, finely chopped
- 1 bunch red or white Swiss chard
- 1 onion, chopped
- 1/4 C. uncooked small pasta, such as orzo or
- 1 clove garlic, minced
- pastina
- 1/4 teaspoons freshly grated nutmeg (optional)
- 5 large fresh sage leaves, minced
- 1/8 teaspoons crushed red pepper flakes
- 5 leaves fresh basil, coarsely chopped (optional) (optional)
- 1 Tablespoons grated Parmesan cheese, divided
- 6 C. chicken broth, or more as needed(optional)
- 1 (15 oz.) can cannellini beans, drained and
- 1 Tablespoons extra-virgin olive oil, divided (optional) rinsed - or more to taste
- 2 Tablespoons chopped sun-dried tomatoes
- 2 oz. Parmesan cheese rind

Directions

a) Place a large saucepan on medium heat. Add the bacon, onion, garlic, nutmeg, and red pepper flakes then cook them for 5 min.

b) Stir in the chicken broth and cannellini beans then cook them until they start boiling. Add the sun-dried tomatoes and the piece of Parmesan cheese rind.

c) Cook the soup on low heat for 10 min.

d) Slice the stems of the chard into 3/4-inch ling and the leaves into 1-inch-wide slices. Add the stems with pasta to the soup then cook them for 10 min on low heat.

e) Add the sliced chard leaves, sage, and basil then cook it for 5 min on low heat. Serve the soup warm with cheese.

16. Cheesy Chicken Cream Pasta

SERVES 6

Ingredients

- 1 1/2 C. flour, plus
- 1 red pepper, julienne cut
- 1 Tablespoons flour
- 1/2 C. white wine
- 1 Tablespoons salt
- 1/2 lb. whole spinach leaves, stemmed
- 2 teaspoons black pepper
- 12 fluid oz. heavy cream
- 2 teaspoons Italian herb seasoning
- 1 C. parmesan cheese, grated
- 3 lbs. boneless skinless chicken breasts
- 3 fluid oz. vegetable oil, divided
- 1 lb. penne pasta
- 1 Tablespoons garlic, chopped

Directions

a) Before you do anything set the oven to 350 F.

b) Get a shallow dish: Mix in it 1 1/2 C. flour, salt, black pepper, and Italian herb seasoning.

c) Place a large oven-proof skillet on medium heat then heat in it some oil.

d) Coat the chicken breasts with the flour mix then brown it in the skillet for 4 min on each side. Transfer the skillet with chicken to the oven and cook it for 17 min.

e) Cook the penne pasta by following the directions on the package until it becomes dente.

f) Drain it and place it aside.

g) To make the sauce:

h) Place a large saucepan on medium heat. Add to it 1 oz. of oil. Cook in it the red pepper with garlic for 1 min. Stir in the flour.

i) Stir in the wine and coo them for 1 min. Add the cream and spinach then cook them until they start boiling. Stir in the cheese until it melts.

j) Get a large mixing bowl: Toss the pasta with 1/2 of the sauce. Serve the pasta warm with chicken then drizzle the remaining sauce on top.

17. Classical Alfredo

SERVES 8

Ingredients

- 6 skinless, boneless chicken breast halves
- 3/4 teaspoons ground white pepper
- 3 C. milk
- 6 Tablespoons butter, divided
- 1 C. half-and-half
- 4 cloves garlic, minced, divided
- 3/4 C. grated Parmesan cheese
- 1 Tablespoons Italian seasoning
- 8 oz. shredded Monterey Jack cheese
- 1 lb. fettuccini pasta
- 3 Roma (plum) tomatoes, diced
- 1 onion, diced
- 1/2 C. sour cream
- 1 (8 oz.) package sliced mushrooms
- 1/3 C. all-purpose flour
- 1 Tablespoons salt

Directions

a) Stir your chicken after coating it with Italian seasoning in 2 Tablespoons of butter with 2 pieces of garlic.

b) Stir fry the meat until it is fully done then place everything to the side.

c) Now boil your pasta in water and salt for 9 Minutes then remove all the liquids.

d) At the same time stir fry your onions in 4 Tablespoons of butter along with the mushrooms and 2 more pieces of garlic.

e) Continue frying the mix until the onions are see-through then combine in your pepper, salt, and flour.

f) Stir and cook the mix for 4 Minutes. Then gradually add in your half and a half and the milk, while stirring until everything is smooth.

g) Combine in the Monterey and parmesan and let the mix cook until the cheese has melted then add the chicken, sour cream, and tomatoes.

h) Serve your pasta topped liberally with the chicken mix and sauce.

18. Easy Italian Parmigiana

SERVES 2

Ingredients

- 1 egg, beaten
- 2 oz. shredded mozzarella cheese
- 2 oz. dry bread crumbs
- 1/4 C. grated Parmesan cheese
- 2 skinless, boneless chicken breast halves
- 3/4 (16 oz.) jar spaghetti sauce

Directions

a) Coat a cookie sheet with oil then set your oven to 350 degrees before doing anything else.

b) Get a bowl and add in your eggs.

c) Get the 2nd bowl and add in your bread crumbs.

d) Coat your chicken first with the eggs then with the bread crumbs.

e) Lay your pieces of chicken on the cookie sheet and cook them in the oven for 45 minutes, until they are fully done.

f) Now add half of your pasta sauce to a casserole dish and lay in your chicken on top of the sauce.

g) Place the rest of the sauce on top of the chicken pieces. Then add a topping of parmesan and mozzarella over everything.

h) Cook the parmigiana in the oven for 25 Minutes.

15. Chicken from Milan

SERVES 4

INGREDIENTS

- 1 Tablespoons butter
- salt and pepper to taste
- 2 cloves garlic, minced
- 2 Tablespoons vegetable oil
- 1/2 C. sun-dried tomatoes, diced
- 2 Tablespoons diced fresh basil
- 1 C. chicken broth, divided
- 8 oz. dry fettuccini pasta
- 1 C. heavy cream
- 1 lb. skinless, boneless chicken breast
- halves

Directions

a) Coat a cookie sheet with oil then set your oven to 350 degrees before doing anything else.

b) Stir fry your garlic for 1 min, in butter, then combine in 3/4 C. of broth and the tomatoes.

c) Turn up the heat and get everything boiling.

d) Once the mix is boiling, set the heat to low, and let the contents cook for 12 Minutes.

e) Now add in the cream and get everything boiling again until the mix is thick.

f) Coat your chicken all over with pepper and salt then fry the meat in hot oil for 5 minutes on each side until fully done. Then place the chicken to the side in a covered bowl.

g) Remove some of the drippings from the pan and begin to get 1/4 C. of broth boiling while scraping the bottom bits.

h) Once the mix is boiling, set the heat to low, add in the basil, and let the broth reduce a bit.

i) Once it has been reduced, combine it with the tomato cream sauce.

j) Now begin to boil your pasta in water and salt for 9 minutes then remove the liquid and place everything in a bowl. Stir the pasta with about 5 Tablespoons of tomato cream sauce.

k) Now slice your chicken into strips and get the tomato hot again. Divide your noodles between serving dishes. Top the noodles with some chicken and then some sauce.

16. Nutty Chicken Pasta

SERVES 4

Ingredients

- 6 slices bacon
- 1 (6 oz.) jar marinated artichoke hearts, drained
- 10 asparagus spears, ends trimmed and coarsely chopped
- 1/2 (16 oz.) package rotini, elbow, or penne
- 1 cooked chicken breast, cubed pasta
- 1/4 C. dried cranberries
- 3 Tablespoons low-fat mayonnaise
- 1/4 C. toasted sliced almonds
- 3 Tablespoons balsamic vinaigrette salad dressing
- salt and pepper to taste
- 2 teaspoons lemon juice
- 1 teaspoons Worcestershire sauce

Directions

a) Place a large pan over medium heat. Cook in it the bacon until it becomes crisp. Remove it from the excess grease. Crumble it and place it aside.

b) Cook the pasta according to the directions on the package.

c) Get a small mixing bowl: Combine in it the mayo, balsamic vinaigrette, lemon juice, and Worcestershire sauce. Mix them well.

d) Get a large mixing bowl: Toss in it the pasta with dressing. Add the artichoke, chicken, cranberries, almonds, crumbled bacon, and asparagus, a pinch of salt and pepper.

e) Stir them well. Chill the salad in the fridge for 1 h 10 min then serve it.

17. Chicken Tenders and Farfalle Salad

SERVES 6

Ingredients

- 6 eggs
- 3 green onions, thinly sliced
- 1 (16 oz.) package farfalle (bow-tie) Pasta
- 1/2 red onion, chopped
- 1/2 (16 oz.) bottle Italian-style salad
- 6 chicken tenders

Dressing

- 1 cucumber, sliced
- 4 romaine lettuce hearts, thinly sliced
- 1 bunch radishes, trimmed and sliced
- 2 carrots, peeled and sliced

Directions

a) Place the eggs in a large saucepan and cover them with water. Cook the eggs over medium heat until they start boiling.

b) Turn off the heat and let the eggs sit for 16 min. Rinse the eggs with some cold water to make them lose heat.

c) Peel the eggs and slice them then place them aside.

d) Place the chicken tenders in a large saucepan. Cover them with 1/4 C. of water. Cook them over medium heat until the chicken is done.

e) Drain the chicken tenders and cut them into small pieces.

f) Get a large mixing bowl: Toss in it the pasta, chicken, eggs, cucumber, radishes, carrots, green onions, and red onion. Add the Italian dressing and mix them again.

g) Place the salad in the fridge for 1 h 15 min.

h) Place lettuce hearts on serving plates. Divide the salad between them.

18.   Chicken Alfredo Lasagna

Ingredients

- 4 ounces thinly sliced pancetta, cut into strips
- 3 ounces thinly sliced prosciutto or deli ham, cut into strips
- 3 cups shredded rotisserie chicken
- 5 tablespoons unsalted butter, cubed
- 1/4 cup all-purpose flour
- 4 cups whole milk
- 2 cups shredded Asiago cheese, divided
- 2 tablespoons minced fresh parsley, divided
- 1/4 teaspoon coarsely ground pepper
- Pinch ground nutmeg
- 9 no-cook lasagna noodles
- 1-1/2 cups shredded part-skim mozzarella cheese
- 1-1/2 cups shredded Parmesan cheese

Directions

a) In a large skillet, cook pancetta and prosciutto over medium heat until browned. Drain on paper towels. Transfer to a large bowl; add chicken and toss to combine.

b) For sauce, in a large saucepan, melt butter over medium heat. Stir in flour until smooth; gradually whisk in milk. Bring to a boil, stirring constantly; cook and stir 1-2 minutes or until thickened. Remove from heat; stir in 1/2 cup Asiago cheese, 1 tablespoon parsley, pepper and nutmeg.

c) Preheat oven to 375°. Spread 1/2 cup sauce into a greased 13x9-in. baking dish. Layer with a third of each of the following: noodles, sauce, meat mixture, Asiago, mozzarella and Parmesan cheeses. Repeat layers twice.

d) Bake, covered, 30 minutes. Uncover; bake 15 minutes longer or until bubbly. Sprinkle with remaining parsley. Let stand 10 minutes before serving.

19. Chicken Tetrazzini

Ingredient

- 8 ounces uncooked spaghetti
- 2 teaspoons plus 3 tablespoons butter, divided
- 8 bacon strips, chopped
- 2 cups sliced fresh mushrooms
- 1 small onion, chopped
- 1 small green pepper, chopped
- 1/3 cup all-purpose flour
- 1/4 teaspoon salt
- 1/4 teaspoon pepper
- 3 cups chicken broth
- 3 cups coarsely shredded rotisserie chicken
- 2 cups frozen peas (about 8 ounces)
- 1 jar (4 ounces) diced pimientos, drained
- 1/2 cup grated Romano or Parmesan cheese

Directions

a) Preheat oven to 375°. Cook spaghetti according to package directions for al dente. Drain; transfer to a greased 13x9-in. baking dish. Add 2 teaspoons butter and toss to coat.

b) Meanwhile, in a large skillet, cook bacon over medium heat until crisp, stirring occasionally. Remove with a slotted spoon; drain on paper towels. Discard drippings, reserving 1 tablespoon in pan. Add mushrooms, onion and green pepper to drippings; cook and stir over medium-high heat 5-7 minutes or until tender. Remove from pan.

c) In same pan, heat remaining butter over medium heat. Stir in flour, salt and pepper until smooth; gradually whisk in broth. Bring to a boil, stirring occasionally; cook and stir 3-5 minutes or until slightly thickened. Add chicken, peas, pimientos and mushroom mixture; heat through, stirring occasionally. Spoon over spaghetti. Sprinkle with bacon and cheese.

d) Bake, uncovered, 25-30 minutes or until golden brown. Let stand 10 minutes before serving.

20.   Angel Hair Shrimp Bake

Ingredient

- 1 package (9 ounces) refrigerated angel hair pasta
- 1-1/2 pounds uncooked medium shrimp, peeled and deveined
- 3/4 cup crumbled feta cheese
- 1/2 cup shredded Swiss cheese
- 1 jar (16 ounces) chunky salsa
- 1/2 cup shredded Monterey Jack cheese
- 3/4 cup minced fresh parsley
- 1 teaspoon dried basil
- 1 teaspoon dried oregano
- 2 large eggs
- 1 cup half-and-half cream
- 1 cup plain yogurt
- Chopped fresh parsley, optional

Directions

a) In a greased 13x9-in. baking dish, layer half the pasta, shrimp, feta cheese, Swiss cheese and salsa. Repeat layers. Sprinkle with the Monterey Jack cheese, parsley, basil and oregano.

b) In a small bowl, whisk the eggs, cream and yogurt; pour over casserole. Bake, uncovered, at 350° until a thermometer reads 160°, 25-30 minutes. Let stand for 5 minutes before serving. If desired, top with chopped parsley.

21.   Curry Lasagna

Ingredient

- 1 tablespoon canola oil
- 1 medium onion, chopped
- 4 teaspoons curry powder
- 3 garlic cloves, minced
- 1 can (6 ounces) tomato paste
- 2 cans (13.66 ounces each) coconut milk
- 1 pound (about 4 cups) shredded rotisserie chicken, skin removed
- 12 lasagna noodles, uncooked
- 2 cups part-skim ricotta cheese
- 2 large eggs
- 1/2 cup chopped fresh cilantro, divided
- 1 package (10 ounces) frozen chopped spinach, thawed and squeezed dry
- 1/2 teaspoon salt
- 1/4 teaspoon pepper
- 2 cups shredded part-skim mozzarella cheese
- Lime wedges

Directions

a) Preheat oven to 350°. In a large skillet, heat oil over medium-high heat. Add onion; cook and stir until softened, about 5 minutes. Add curry powder and garlic; cook 1 minute more. Stir in tomato paste; pour coconut milk into skillet. Bring to a boil. Reduce heat and simmer 5 minutes. Stir in cooked chicken.

b) Meanwhile, cook lasagna noodles according to package directions. Drain. Combine ricotta, eggs, 1/4 cup cilantro, spinach and seasonings.

c) Spread a fourth of chicken mixture into a 13x9-in. baking dish coated with cooking spray. Layer with 4 noodles, half the ricotta mixture, a fourth of chicken mixture and 1/2 cup mozzarella. Repeat layers. Top with remaining noodles, remaining chicken mixture and remaining mozzarella.

d) Bake, uncovered, until bubbly, 40-45 minutes. Cool 10 minutes before cutting. Top with remaining cilantro; serve with lime wedges.

22. Baked rigatoni and meatballs

Ingredient

- 3½ cup Rigatoni pasta
- 1⅓ cup Mozzarella, shredded
- 3 tablespoons Parmesan, freshly grated
- 1 pounds Lean ground turkey

Directions:

a) Meatballs: In bowl, beat egg lightly; mix in onion, crumbs, garlic, Parmesan, oregano, salt and pepper. Mix in turkey.

b) Shape heaping tablespoonful into balls.

c) In large skillet, heat oil over medium-high heat; cook meatballs, in batches if necessary, for 8-10 minutes or until browned on all sides.

d) Add onion, garlic, mushrooms, green pepper, basil, sugar, oregano, salt, pepper and water to skillet; cook over medium heat, stirring occasionally, for about 10 minutes or until vegetables are softened. Stir in tomatoes and tomato paste; bring to boil. Add meatballs

e) Meanwhile, in large pot of boiling salted water, cook rigatoni. Transfer to 11x7-inch baking dish or 8-cup shallow oven casserole.

f) Sprinkle mozzarella, then Parmesan evenly over top. Bake

23. Baked penne with turkey meatballs

Ingredient

- 1 pounds Ground turkey
- 1 large Garlic clove; minced
- ¾ cup Fresh bread crumbs
- ½ cup Finely chopped onion
- 3 tablespoons Pine nuts; toasted
- ½ cup Minced fresh parsley leaves
- 1 large Egg; beaten lightly
- 1 teaspoon Salt
- 1 teaspoon Black pepper
- 4 tablespoons Olive oil
- 1 pounds Penne
- 1½ cup Coarsely grated mozzarella cheese
- 1 cup Freshly grated Romano cheese
- 6 cups Tomato sauce
- 1 Container; (15 oz.) ricotta cheese

Directions:

a) In a bowl, stir together well turkey, garlic, bread crumbs, onion, pine nuts, parsley, egg, salt, and pepper and form into meatballs and cook.

b) Cook pasta

c) In a small bowl toss together mozzarella and Romano. Spoon about 1½ cups tomato sauce and half of meatballs into prepared dish and spoon half of pasta on top.

d) Spread half remaining sauce and half cheese mixture over pasta. Top with remaining meatballs and drop dollops of ricotta over meatballs. Bake penne in middle of oven 30 to 35 minutes.

FISH/SEAFOOD PASTA

24. Pesto Shrimp with Pasta

Servings Size: 4

Ingredients
- 8 oz. spaghetti
- 2 minced garlic cloves
- Salt to taste
- 1 Tablespoons olive oil
- 8 oz. asparagus
- 1 cup sliced white mushrooms
- $\frac{3}{4}$ pound peeled and deveined shrimp
- $\frac{1}{8}$ teaspoons red pepper
- $\frac{1}{4}$ cup pesto – or prepare your own
- 2 Tablespoons grated parmesan cheese

Directions
a) Place the spaghetti in a pot of boiling salted water and cook for 10 minutes.
b) Drain the spaghetti but keep some of the pasta water aside.
c) Heat the olive oil in a skillet.
d) Sauté the garlic, asparagus and mushrooms for 5 minutes or until they are tender.
e) Add the shrimp to the skillet and season with red pepper
f) Cook for 5 minutes.
g) If liquid is needed, add a few tablespoons of pasta water.
h) Combine the pesto sauce and the parmesan cheese.
i) Stir the pesto into the shrimp.
j) Cook for 5 minutes
k) Serve over the spaghetti.

25.   Macaroni Seafood Salad

Servings Size: 12

Ingredients
- 16 oz. farfalle pasta
- 3 chopped hard-boiled eggs
- 2 chopped celery sticks
- 6 oz., cooked small shrimp
- $\frac{1}{2}$ cup real crab meat
- Salt and pepper to taste

Dressing:
- 1 cup mayonnaise
- $\frac{1}{2}$ teaspoons paprika
- 2 teaspoons lemon juice

Directions
a) Cook the pasta in a pot of salted boiling water for 10 minutes. Drain.
b) Transfer the pasta to a large bowl and stir in the remaining salad ingredients.
c) Combine the dressing ingredients and toss with the salad.
d) Cover and refrigerate for 1 hour.

26.   Smoked Salmon Pasta

Servings Size: 8

Ingredients
- 16 oz. penne pasta
- $\frac{1}{4}$ cup butter
- 1 small, chopped onion
- 3 minced garlic cloves
- 3 Tablespoons flour
- 2 cups light cream
- $\frac{1}{2}$ cup white wine
- 1 Tablespoons lemon juice
- $\frac{1}{2}$ cup grated Romano cheese
- 1 cup sliced mushrooms
- $\frac{3}{4}$ lb. chopped smoked salmon

Directions
a) Cook the pasta in a pot of salted water for 10 minutes. Drain.
b) Melt butter in a skillet and sauté the onion and garlic for 5 minutes.
c) Stir the flour into the butter mixture and keep stirring for 2 minutes.
d) Gently add the light cream.
e) Bring the liquid just below the boiling point.
f) Stir in the cheese and keep stirring until the mixture is smooth, about 3 minutes.
g) Add the mushrooms and simmer for 5 minutes.
h) Transfer the salmon to the skillet and cook for 3 minutes.
i) Serve the salmon mixture over the penne pasta.

27. Bay Scallops with Spaghetti

Servings Size: 4

Ingredients
- 8 oz. spaghetti
- ⅓ cup dry white wine
- 3 Tablespoons butter
- 1 lb. bay scallops
- 4 minced garlic cloves
- 1 pinch red pepper flakes
- 1 cup heavy cream
- Salt and pepper to taste
- Juice of half a lemon
- ¼ cup grated Pecorino-Romano

Directions
a) Cook the spaghetti in a pot of salted water for 10 minutes. Drain and set aside.
b) Heat the butter in a large skillet.
c) Add the scallops in a single layer and brown for 2 minutes on medium heat.
d) Turn the scallops and brown the other side for 1 more minute.
e) Stir in the garlic, red pepper flakes, and wine and cook for 1 minute. Be sure not to overcook the scallops.
f) Season with salt, pepper, and the juice of half a lemon.
g) Stir the spaghetti into the skillet and combine it with the scallops.
h) Simmer for 2 minutes and top with the grated cheese.

28. Crab Salad

Servings Size: 4

Ingredients
- 1 cup elbow macaroni
- ½ cup mayonnaise
- 3 Tablespoons sour cream
- 12 oz. flaked crab meat
- 3 chopped celery stalks
- ¼ cup thawed frozen pea
- 1 teaspoons lemon juice
- ¾ teaspoons Old Bay seasoning
- Salt and pepper to taste
- ½ teaspoons paprika - optional

Directions
a) Cook the macaroni in a pot of salted water for 10 minutes and drain. Let cool.
b) Combine the remaining ingredients and stir in the macaroni.
c) Top with paprika, if using.

29. Shrimp Lo Mein

Servings Size: 2

Ingredients
- 8 oz. spaghetti
- $\frac{1}{4}$ cup soy sauce
- 3 Tablespoons oyster sauce
- 1 Tablespoons honey
- $\frac{1}{2}$ inch nob of grated ginger
- 1 Tablespoons olive oil
- 1 chopped red bell pepper
- 1 sliced small onion
- $\frac{1}{2}$ cup chopped water chestnuts
- $\frac{1}{2}$ cup sliced cremini mushrooms
- 3 minced garlic cloves
- 1 lb. peeled and deveined fresh shrimp
- 2 beaten eggs

Directions
a) Cook the spaghetti in a pot of salted water for 10 minutes. Drain the water.
b) Combine the soy sauce, oyster sauce, honey, and ginger in a bowl.
c) Heat the olive oil in a large skillet.
d) Sauté the bell pepper, onion, water chestnuts, mushrooms for 5 minutes.
e) Stir in the garlic and shrimp and stir for 2 more minutes.
f) Move the ingredients to one side of the skillet and scramble the eggs on the other side for 5 minutes.
g) Add the spaghetti and sauce and combine all ingredients for 2 minutes.

30. Shrimp Carbonara

Servings Size: 6

Ingredients
- ¼ cup olive oil, divided
- 1 lb. chicken cubes
- 4 Tablespoons minced garlic, divided
- 1 teaspoons thyme
- 1 teaspoons oregano
- 1 teaspoons basil
- 1 lb. peeled and deveined shrimp
- 16 oz. linguine
- 6 sliced diced bacon
- Salt and pepper to taste
- 1 chopped onion
- 1 cup sliced mushrooms
- 1 chopped red bell pepper
- 2 cup heavy cream
- 1 cup milk
- 1 ½ cups grated Parmesan cheese
- 2 egg yolks
- 1 cup white wine.

Directions
a) Heat 2 Tablespoons olive in a large pan.
b) Sauté half the garlic and season with thyme, oregano, and basil.
c) Stir in the chicken and cook on low for 10 minutes.
d) Place the chicken on a platter and set aside.
e) Using the same pan, heat 2 Tablespoons olive oil and sauté the remaining garlic for 2 minutes.
f) Stir in the shrimp and cook on low for 6 minutes.

g) Transfer the shrimp with the chicken.
h) Cook the linguine in a pot of salted water for 12 minutes.
i) Again, using the same pan, fry the bacon until done, about 5 minutes.
j) Drain the bacon on a paper towel and crumble. Set aside.
k) Sauté the onion, bell pepper, and mushroom in the pan with the bacon fat for 5 minutes.
l) Combine the heavy cream, milk, parmesan cheese, egg yolks, salt, and pepper in a bowl.
m) Add the wine to the onion, pepper, and mushroom in the pan and bring to a boil.
n) Cook on low for 5 minutes.
o) Stir in the heavy cream mixture and simmer for 5 minutes.
p) Return the shrimp and chicken to the pan and coat with the sauce.
q) Serve the shrimp and chicken with the pasta.

31.   Lobster Mac and Cheese

Servings Size: 2

Ingredients
- 1 Tablespoons olive oil
- 3 lobster tails, split in half lengthwise and deveined
- 3 Tablespoons butter
- 2 Tablespoons flour
- 1 $\frac{1}{2}$ cups half and half
- $\frac{1}{2}$ cup milk
- $\frac{1}{4}$ teaspoons paprika
- $\frac{1}{4}$ teaspoons chili powder
- Salt to taste
- $\frac{1}{4}$ teaspoons Worcestershire sauce
- $\frac{1}{2}$ cup grated Cheddar cheese
- 3 Tablespoons, grated Gruyere cheese
- 1 cup prepared elbow macaroni
- $\frac{1}{2}$ cup Panko breadcrumbs
- $\frac{1}{4}$ cup melted butter
- 5 Tablespoons grated Parmesan cheese

Directions
a) Preheat the oven to 400 degrees.
b) Coat two gratin dishes with non-stick spray
c) Heat the oil in a skillet and brown the lobster tails for 2 minutes on medium heat.
d) Let the lobsters cool and separate the meat from the shells.
e) Chop the meat and discard the shells.
f) Use the same skillet to melt the butter.
g) Create a roux by stirring in the flour and continue stirring for 1 minute.

h) Pour in the half and half and milk and continue stirring for 3 minutes.
i) Let the liquid simmer and add the paprika, chili powder, salt, and Worcestershire Sauce.
j) Let simmer for 4 minutes.
k) Add the cheddar and Gruyere cheeses and stir for 5 minutes, until the cheese is melted.
l) Add the macaroni to the cheese sauce and gently stir in the lobster chunks.
m) Fill both gratin dishes with the mac and cheese mixture.
n) Combine the Panko, melted butter, and parmesan cheese in a bowl.
o) Drizzle the mixture over the mac and cheese.
p) Bake the mac and cheese for 15 minutes.

36. Tuna Pasta

SERVES 4

Ingredients

- 2 Tablespoons olive oil
- 1 (7 oz.) can oil-packed tuna, drained
- 1 anchovy fillet
- 1/4 C. diced fresh flat-leaf parsley
- 2 Tablespoons capers
- 1 (12 oz.) package spaghetti
- 3 cloves minced garlic
- 1 Tablespoons extra-virgin olive oil, or to taste
- 1/2 C. dry white wine
- 1/4 C. freshly grated Parmigiano-Reggiano
- 1/4 teaspoons dried oregano
- cheese, or to taste
- 1 pinch red pepper flakes, or to taste
- 1 Tablespoons diced fresh flat-leaf parsley, or to taste 3 C. crushed Italian (plum) tomatoes
- salt and ground black pepper to taste
- 1 pinch cayenne pepper, or to taste

Directions

a) Stir fry your capers and anchovies in olive oil for 4 Minutes then combine in the garlic and continue frying the mix for 2 more minutes.

b) Now add pepper flakes, white wine, and orange.

c) Stir the mix and turn up the heat.

d) Let the mix cook for 5 minutes before adding the tomatoes and getting the mix to a gentle simmer.

e) Once the mix is simmering add-in: cayenne, black pepper, and salt.

f) Set the heat to low and let everything cook for 12 Minutes.

g) Now begin to boil your pasta in water and salt for 10 Minutes then remove all the liquids and leave the noodles in the pan.

h) Combine the simmering tomatoes with the noodles and place a lid on the pot. With a low level of heat warm everything for 4 Minutes.

i) When serving your pasta top, it with some Parmigiano-Reggiano, parsley, and olive oil.

37. Shrimp Scampi

Servings Size: 2

Ingredients
- 1 lb. peeled and deveined large shrimp
- ½ teaspoons garlic powder
- ½ teaspoons Old Bay seasoning
- 8 oz. angel hair pasta
- ¼ cup butter
- 5 minced garlic cloves
- 3 Tablespoons white wine
- 1 Tablespoons lemon juice
- ½ cup half-and-half
- 3 Tablespoons chopped parsley
- 1 teaspoon red pepper flakes

Directions
a) Place the shrimp in a bowl and toss with the garlic powder and Old Bay seasoning. Let sit for 10 minutes.
b) Cook the angel hair pasta in a pot of salted water for 5 minutes. It should be al dente. Drain the water.
c) Melt the butter in a skillet.
d) Add the garlic and sauté for 1 minute
e) Stir in the shrimp and sauté for 2 minutes each side – not any longer.
f) Add the butter, wine, lemon juice, and half and half and stir for 2 minutes.
g) Place the angel hair pasta in a bowl and top with the shrimp and sauce.
h) Drizzle with the red pepper flakes and chopped parsley before serving.

38. Classical Penne Pasta

SERVES 8

Ingredients

- 1 (16 oz.) package penne pasta
- 2 (14.5 oz.) cans diced tomatoes
- 2 Tablespoons olive oil
- 1 lb. shrimp, peeled and deveined
- 1/4 C. diced red onion
- 1 C. grated Parmesan cheese
- 1 Tablespoons diced garlic
- 1/4 C. white wine

Directions

a) Boil your pasta in water and salt for 9 minutes then remove the liquids.

b) Now begin to stir fry your garlic and onions in oil until the onions are soft.

c) Then add in the tomatoes and wine.

d) Simmer the mix for 12 minutes while stirring. Then add in the shrimp and cook everything for 6 Minutes.

e) Now add the pasta and stir everything to evenly coat the noodles.

39. Linguine and Clam Sauce

Servings Size: 4

Ingredients
- 16 oz. linguini
- 1 Tablespoons olive oil
- 1 chopped onion
- 5 minced garlic cloves
- ½ cup butter
- Salt and pepper to taste
- ¼ cup dry white wine
- ¼ cup clam juice
- 1 ½ cups chopped clams
- 1 teaspoon red pepper flakes

Directions
a) Cook the linguini in a pot of salted water for 10 minutes. Drain.
b) Heat the olive oil in a skillet and sauté the onion and garlic for 5 minutes.
c) Add the butter, salt, pepper, wine, and clam juice.
d) Simmer for 25 minutes. The sauce should be reduced and thickened.
e) Stir in the clams and simmer for 5 minutes.
f) Place the linguini in a bowl and cover with the clam sauce.
g) Serve topped with red pepper flakes.

MEAT PASTA

40. Bolognese Sauce

Servings. 10

Ingredients
- 1 Tablespoons olive oil
- 3 oz. cut-up pancetta
- 1 chopped onion
- 2 minced garlic cloves
- 1 cup sliced mushrooms
- 2 shredded carrots
- 2 chopped celery stalks
- 1 lb. ground beef
- ¾ lb. ground pork
- 28 oz. crushed canned tomatoes
- 6 oz. tomato paste
- ½ cup dry white wine
- ¾ cup stock
- ½ cup milk
- 1 teaspoons Italian seasoning or to taste
- Salt and pepper to taste
- ¼ cup grated Pecorino Romano
- 1 lb. prepared pasta

Directions
a) Heat the oil in a large skillet and sauté the pancetta, onion, and garlic for 5 minutes.
b) Use the skillet the brown both meats for 5 minutes.
c) Drain off any fat.
d) Add the pancetta mixture back to the skillet and stir in the beef and pork.
e) Stir in the remaining ingredients and combine well.

f) Cover the skillet and simmer for 1 hour while frequently stirring.
g) Serve over the cooked pasta.

41.Beef Stroganoff

Servings Size: 4

Ingredients
- 1 ½ lb. ground beef
- 1 small onion
- 3 minced garlic cloves
- 1 cup sliced mushrooms
- 1 (10.5 oz.) can condensed cream of mushroom soup
- 1 (10.5 oz.) can beef broth
- 2 teaspoons Worcestershire sauce
- 2 Tablespoons sherry
- 3 Tablespoons dry Ranch dressing mix
- Salt and pepper to taste
- ½ cup sour cream – taste it and add more if you want
- 8 oz. cooked egg noodles

Directions
a) Prepare the egg noodles in boiling salted water for 5 minutes and set aside.
b) Brown the beef in a large skillet or pot for 5 minutes.
c) Stir in the onion, garlic and mushrooms and sauté for another 5 minutes.
d) Drain any fat.
e) Pour in the cream of mushroom soup, broth, Worcestershire sauce, sherry, dry Ranch dressing and season with salt and pepper.
f) Simmer for 20 minutes.
g) Stir in the sour cream and simmer for 5 more minutes.
h) Place the egg noodles on a platter and top with the beef stroganoff.

42. Saucy Beef Skillet

SERVES 6

Ingredients

- 500 g minced beef
- 1 Tablespoons beef stock, dried instant
- 4 Tablespoons olive oil
- 2 bay leaves
- 1 onion, finely diced
- Worcestershire sauce, dash
- 2 garlic cloves, peeled and crushed
- 1 teaspoons allspice
- 1 teaspoons cinnamon
- 1 teaspoon paprika
- 130 g tomato paste
- 500 g pasta sauce

Directions

a) Place a large pan on high heat. Heat the oil in it. Add the onion, garlic, beef, and spices then cook them for 6 min.

b) Stir in the tomato and pasta sauce, paprika, beef stock, bay leaves, salt, and pepper then cook them for 30 min on low heat while stirring often.

c) Serve your saucy beef warm with some pasta.

43. Classical Lasagna

SERVES 8

Ingredients

- 1 1/2 lbs. lean ground beef
- 2 eggs, beaten
- 1 onion, diced
- 1-pint part-skim ricotta cheese
- 2 cloves garlic, minced
- 1/2 C. grated Parmesan cheese
- 1 Tablespoons diced fresh basil
- 2 Tablespoons dried parsley
- 1 teaspoons dried oregano
- 1 teaspoons salt
- 2 Tablespoons brown sugar
- 1 lb. mozzarella cheese, shredded
- 1 1/2 teaspoons salt
- 2 Tablespoons grated Parmesan cheese
- 1 (29 oz.) can diced tomatoes
- 2 (6 oz.) cans tomato paste
- 12 dry lasagna noodles

Directions

a) Stir fry your garlic, onions, and beef for 3 Minutes then combine in tomato paste, basil, diced tomatoes, oregano, 1.5 teaspoons salt, and brown sugar.

b) Now set your oven to 375 degrees before doing anything else.

c) Begin to boil your pasta in water and salt for 9 Minutes then remove all the liquids.

d) Get a bowl, combine 1 teaspoons salt, eggs, parsley, ricotta, and parmesan.

e) Place a third of the pasta in a casserole dish and top everything with half of the cheese mix, one-third of the sauce, and 1/2 of the mozzarella.

f) Continue layering in this manner until all the ingredients have been used up.

g) Then top everything with some more parmesan.

h) Cook the lasagna in the oven for 35 Minutes.

44. Saucy Cheddar Fusilli Salad

SERVES 10

Ingredients

- 2 Tablespoons olive oil
- 6 green onions, chopped
- 1 teaspoons salt
- 3/4 C. chopped pickled jalapeno peppers
- 1 (16 oz.) package fusilli pasta
- 1 (2.25 oz.) can slice black olives
- 2 lb. extra lean ground beef
- (optional)
- 1 (1.25 oz.) package taco seasoning mix
- 1 (8 oz.) package shredded Cheddar
- 1 (24 oz.) jar mild salsa
- cheese
- 1 (8 oz.) bottle ranch dressing
- 1 1/2 red bell peppers, chopped

Directions

a) 1. Place a large pot over medium heat. Fill it with water and stir into it the olive oil with salt.

b) Cook it until it starts boiling.

c) 2. Add the pasta and boil it for 10 min. Remove it from the water and place it aside to drain.

d) 3. Place a large pan over medium heat. Brown in it the beef for 12 min. Discard the excess grease.

e) 4. Add the taco seasoning and mix them well. Place the mix aside to lose heat completely.

f) 5. Get a large mixing bowl: Mix in it the salsa, ranch dressing, bell peppers, green onions, jalapenos, and black olives.

g) 6. Add the pasta with cooked beef, Cheddar cheese, and dressing mix. Stir them well. Place a piece of plastic wrap over the salad bowl. Place it in the fridge for 1 h 15 min.

45.Penne Beef Bake

Ingredient

- 1 package (12 ounces) whole wheat penne pasta
- 1-pound lean ground beef (90% lean)
- 2 medium zucchini, finely chopped
- 1 large green pepper, finely chopped
- 1 small onion, finely chopped
- 1 jar (24 ounces) spaghetti sauce
- 1-1/2 cups reduced-fat Alfredo sauce
- 1 cup shredded part-skim mozzarella cheese, divided
- 1/4 teaspoon garlic powder
- Minced fresh parsley, optional

Directions

a) Cook penne according to package directions. Meanwhile, in a Dutch oven, cook the beef, zucchini, pepper and onion over medium heat until meat is no longer pink, breaking it into crumbles; drain. Stir in the spaghetti sauce, Alfredo sauce, 1/2 cup mozzarella cheese and garlic powder. Drain penne; stir into meat mixture.

b) Transfer to a 13x9-in. baking dish coated with cooking spray. Cover and bake at 375° for 20 minutes. Sprinkle with remaining mozzarella cheese. Bake, uncovered, 3-5 minutes longer or until cheese is melted. If desired, top with parsley.

46. Chili Mac Casserole

Ingredient

- 1 cup uncooked elbow macaroni
- 2 pounds lean ground beef (90% lean)
- 1 medium onion, chopped
- 2 garlic cloves, minced
- 1 can (28 ounces) diced tomatoes, undrained
- 1 can (16 ounces) kidney beans, rinsed and drained
- 1 can (6 ounces) tomato paste
- 1 can (4 ounces) chopped green chiles
- 1-1/4 teaspoons salt
- 1 teaspoon chili powder
- 1/2 teaspoon ground cumin
- 1/2 teaspoon pepper
- 2 cups shredded reduced-fat Mexican cheese blend
- Thinly sliced green onions, optional

Directions

a) Cook macaroni according to package directions. Meanwhile, in a large nonstick skillet, cook the beef, onion and garlic over medium heat until meat is no longer pink, breaking meat into crumbles; drain. Stir in the tomatoes, beans, tomato paste, chiles and seasonings. Drain macaroni; add to beef mixture.

b) Transfer to a 13x9-in. baking dish coated with cooking spray. Cover and bake at 375° until bubbly, 25-30 minutes. Uncover; sprinkle with cheese. Bake until cheese is melted, 5-8 minutes longer. If desired, top with sliced green onions.

47. Three-Cheese Meatball Mostaccioli

Ingredient

- 1 package (16 ounces) mostaccioli
- 2 large eggs, lightly beaten
- 1 carton (15 ounces) part-skim ricotta cheese
- 1-pound ground beef
- 1 medium onion, chopped
- 1 tablespoon brown sugar
- 1 tablespoon Italian seasoning
- 1 teaspoon garlic powder
- 1/4 teaspoon pepper
- 2 jars (24 ounces each) pasta sauce with meat
- 1/2 cup grated Romano cheese
- 1 package (12 ounces) frozen fully cooked Italian meatballs, thawed
- 3/4 cup shaved Parmesan cheese
- Minced fresh parsley or fresh baby arugula, optional

Directions

a) Preheat oven to 350°. Cook mostaccioli according to package directions for al dente; drain. Meanwhile, in a small bowl, mix eggs and ricotta cheese.

b) In a 6-qt. stockpot, cook beef and onion 6-8 minutes or until beef is no longer pink, breaking up beef into crumbles; drain. Stir in brown sugar and seasonings. Add pasta sauce and mostaccioli; toss to combine.

c) Transfer half the pasta mixture to a greased 13x9-in. baking dish. Layer with ricotta mixture and remaining pasta mixture; sprinkle with Romano cheese. Top with meatballs and Parmesan cheese.

d) Bake, uncovered, 35-40 minutes or until heated through. If desired, top with parsley.

48. Baked Ziti

Servings Size: 10

Ingredients
- 1 lb. ziti pasta
- 1 Tablespoons olive oil
- 1 lb. ground beef
- Salt and pepper to taste
- ½ teaspoons garlic salt
- ½ teaspoons garlic powder
- 1 chopped onion
- 6 cups tomato sauce
- ½ teaspoons oregano
- ½ teaspoons basil
- 1 cups ricotta cheese
- 1 beaten egg
- 1 cup. shredded mozzarella cheese
- ¼ cup grated pecorino cheese

Directions
a) Boil the ziti in a pot of salted water for 10 minutes. Drain the water.
b) Heat the olive oil in a pot.
c) Season the beef with salt, pepper, garlic salt, and garlic powder.
d) Brown the meat and the onion in the pot for 5 minutes.
e) Pour in the tomato sauce and season with oregano and basil.
f) Simmer for 25 minutes.
g) Preheat the oven to 350 degrees.
h) Whisk the egg and ricotta cheese together.
i) Sprinkle with the pecorino cheese.
j) Transfer half the pasta and half the sauce to a baking dish.

k) Add half the ricotta cheese.
l) Top with half the mozzarella cheese.
m) Create another layer of pasta, sauce, and mozzarella.
n) Bake for 25 minutes. The cheeses should be bubbly.

49. Easy Spaghetti

Servings Size: 4

Ingredients
- 12 oz. spaghetti
- 1 Tablespoons olive oil
- 1 lb. ground beef
- 1 chopped onion
- 3 minced garlic cloves
- Salt and pepper to taste
- 1 teaspoons sugar
- ¼ teaspoons turmeric
- 2 Tablespoons tomato paste
- 2 cups tomato sauce
- 1 teaspoons Italian seasoning

Directions
a) Prepare the pasta in a pot of boiling salted water for 10 minutes. Drain and set aside.
b) Heat the olive oil in a large skillet.
c) Sauté the onion and garlic for 5 minutes.
d) Stir in the ground beef, salt, pepper, and turmeric and combine well.
e) Add the tomato paste, tomato sauce, and Italian seasoning.
f) Simmer for 45 minutes.
g) Add the spaghetti and toss with the sauce.

50. Hungarian Goulash

Servings Size: 6

Ingredients
- 1 Tablespoons olive oil
- 2 lbs. ground beef
- 2 chopped onions
- 3 minced garlic cloves
- 1 ½ Tablespoons sweet paprika
- Salt and pepper to taste
- 2 Tablespoons Worcestershire sauce
- 2 cups canned diced tomatoes with juices
- ¾ cup red wine
- 1 teaspoons sugar
- ½ teaspoons chili powder
- ¾ cup beef broth
- 2 cups cooked egg noodles

Directions
a) Heat the olive oil in a skillet.
b) Brown the beef, onion, and garlic for 5 minutes.
c) Stir in the paprika, pepper and salt.
d) Add the Worcestershire sauce, diced tomatoes with juices, red wine, sugar, chili powder, and beef broth.
e) Combine well and bring the liquid to a boil.
f) Simmer uncovered for 35 minutes.
g) Check for desired thickness and add more liquid if needed.
h) Serve over the egg noodles.

VEGETABLE PASTA

51. Spinach Lasagna

Servings Size: 8

Ingredients
- 1 Tablespoons olive oil
- 10 oz. chopped frozen spinach
- 1 small, chopped onion
- 1 cup sliced mushrooms
- $\frac{1}{4}$ cup grated parmesan cheese
- 3 minced garlic cloves
- $\frac{3}{4}$ teaspoons Italian seasoning
- 12 oz. shredded mozzarella cheese
- 4 cups of marinara sauce
- 2 cups ricotta cheese
- 2 beaten eggs
- Salt and pepper to taste
- 10 oz. cooked lasagna noodles

Directions
a) Preheat the oven to 350 degrees.
b) Heat the olive oil in a large pot.
c) Sauté the spinach, onion, mushrooms, garlic, and Italian seasoning for 5 minutes.
d) Cover with the marinara sauce and simmer for 30 minutes.
e) Combine the ricotta cheese, mozzarella cheese, parmesan cheese, and the eggs in a bowl.
f) Season with salt and pepper.
g) Pour 1 cup of sauce in the bottom of a lasagna pan.
h) Top with 4 noodles, half the remaining cheese and half the sauce.

i) Repeat the layering and end with the sauce.
j) Cover the pan with aluminum and bake for 55 minutes.
k) Remove the aluminum and cook for 15 more minutes.

52. Provolone Ziti Bake

Ingredient

- 1 tablespoon olive oil
- 1 medium onion, chopped
- 3 garlic cloves, minced
- 2 cans (28 ounces each) Italian crushed tomatoes
- 1-1/2 cups water
- 1/2 cup dry red wine or reduced-sodium broth
- 1 tablespoon sugar
- 1 teaspoon dried basil
- 1 package (16 ounces) ziti or small tube pasta
- 8 slices provolone cheese

Directions

a) Preheat oven to 350°. In a 6-qt. stockpot, heat oil over medium-high heat. Add onion; cook and stir 2-3 minutes or until tender. Add garlic; cook 1 minute longer. Stir in tomatoes, water, wine, sugar and basil. Bring to a boil; remove from heat. Stir in uncooked ziti.

b) Transfer to a 13x9-in. baking dish coated with cooking spray. Bake, covered, 1 hour. Top with cheese. Bake, uncovered, 5-10 minutes longer or until ziti is tender and cheese is melted.

53. Ratatouille lasagna

SERVES 8-10

Ingredients
- Egg Dough
- Extra-virgin olive oil
- 3 garlic cloves, chopped
- 1 cup (237 ml) red wine
- 2 (28-oz. [794-g]) cans crushed
- tomatoes
- 1 bunch basil
- Kosher salt
- Freshly ground black pepper
- Olive oil
- 1 eggplant, peeled and diced small
- 1 green zucchini, diced small
- 1 summer squash, diced small
- 2 tomatoes, diced small
- 4 garlic cloves, sliced
- 1 red onion, thinly sliced
- Kosher salt
- Freshly ground black pepper

- 3 cups (390 g) shredded mozzarella

Directions

a) Preheat the oven to 350°F (177°C) and bring a large pot of salted water to a boil.

b) Dust two sheet pans with semolina flour. To make the pasta, roll out the dough until the sheet is about 1 / 16 -inch (1.6-mm) thick.

c) Cut the rolled-out sheets into 12-inch (30-cm) sections and place them on sheet pans until you have about 20 sheets. Working in batches, drop the sheets into the boiling water and cook until just pliable, about 1 minute. Place on paper towels and pat dry.

d) To make the sauce, in a pot on medium heat, add the extra-virgin olive oil, garlic and sauté for about a minute or until translucent. Add the red wine and let it reduce by half. Then add the crushed tomatoes, basil and salt and pepper. Let it simmer on low for about 30 minutes.

e) To make the filling, in a large sauté pan over high heat, add a drizzle of olive oil, eggplant, zucchini, squash, tomatoes, garlic and red onion. Season with salt and freshly ground black pepper.

f) To assemble, place the sauce on the bottom of a 9 × 13-inch (22.9 × 33-cm) baking dish. Place the pasta sheets down, overlapping them slightly, covering the bottom of the dish. Add the ratatouille evenly over the pasta sheets and sprinkle mozzarella over the top. Add the next layer of pasta sheets in the opposite Directions and repeat these layers until you reach the top or all of the filling has been used. Ladle some sauce evenly over the top sheet and sprinkle with some more mozzarella.

g) Place the lasagna in the oven and cook for about 45 minutes to 1 hour. Allow it to cool for about 10 minutes before cutting and serving.

54. Eggplant cannelloni

SERVES 6-8

Ingredients
- Egg Dough
- Olive oil
- 3 garlic cloves, chopped
- 1 cup (237 ml) red wine
- 2 (28-oz. [794-g]) cans crushed tomatoes
- 1 bunch basil
- Kosher salt
- Freshly ground black pepper
- Olive oil
- 1 eggplant, peeled and diced small
- 4 garlic cloves, sliced
- 3 sprigs rosemary, chopped
- 4 cups (908 g) ricotta cheese
- 1 cup (130 g) shredded mozzarella
- Kosher salt
- Freshly ground black pepper

Directions

a) Preheat the oven to 350°F (177°C) and bring a large pot of salted water to a boil.

b) Dust two sheet pans with semolina flour. To make the pasta, roll out the dough until the sheet is about 1 / 16 -inch (1.6-mm) thick.

c) Cut the rolled-out sheets into 6-inch (15-cm) sections and place them on the sheet pans until you have about 20 sheets. Working in batches, drop the sheets into the boiling water and cook until just pliable, about 1 minute. Place on paper towels and pat dry.

d) To make the filling, in a large sauté pan over high heat, add a drizzle of olive oil, eggplant, garlic and rosemary and cook until soft, about 4 to 5 minutes. Allow to cool and mix in a bowl with the ricotta and mozzarella. Season with salt and freshly ground black pepper.

e) To assemble, place the sauce on the bottom of a 9 × 13-inch (22.9 × 33-cm) baking dish. With the pasta sheet lengthwise, place about 3 tablespoons (45 g) of filling down at the edge closest to you. Carefully roll the pasta away from you, encasing the filling. Place the stuffed cannelloni in a single layer in the baking dish. Place some more sauce on top of the cannelloni and sprinkle with shredded mozzarella.

f) Place the cannelloni in the oven and cook for about 45 minutes.

55. Artichoke Spinach Pasta Sauce

Servings: 8

Ingredients
- 1/2 (13.5 ounce) can chopped spinach
- 1 (16-ounce) jar alfredo sauce
- 1 (14-ounce) can artichoke hearts, drained and chopped
- 1/2 cup shredded mozzarella cheese
- 1/3 cup shredded Parmesan cheese
- 1/4 (8-ounce) package cream cheese, softened
- 2 cloves garlic, chopped
- 1 Roma tomato, diced
- 1/2 cup water

Directions
a) Dice spinach in food processor.
b) Whisk spinach, Alfredo sauce, artichoke hearts, mozzarella cheese, Parmesan cheese, cream cheese, garlic, and tomato in a pot.

56. Eggplant mezzaluna and tomato confit

SERVES 4-6

Ingredients
- Olive oil
- 2 eggplants, peeled and diced
- 3 garlic cloves, minced
- 1 onion, diced
- Kosher salt
- Freshly ground black pepper
- ¼ cup (45 g) Parmigiano-Reggiano
- 1 cup (130 g) grated mozzarella
- 4 plum tomatoes
- Olive oil
- 3 sprigs rosemary
- 3 sprigs thyme
- 1 garlic clove, thinly sliced
- ½ teaspoons sugar
- Kosher salt
- Freshly ground black pepper
- Ravioli Dough
- 2 cups (50 g) basil

- ½ cup (90 g) grated Parmigiano-Reggiano
- 2 garlic cloves
- ¼ cup (32 g) pignoli nuts
- Kosher salt
- Freshly ground black pepper
- ⅔ cup (160 ml) olive oil

Directions

a) Preheat oven to 325°F (163°C).

b) In a large sauté pan, over medium-high heat, add a drizzle of olive oil, eggplant, garlic, onion, salt and freshly ground black pepper. Cook until the eggplant is soft, about 8 minutes. Remove from the heat and allow it to cool. In a bowl mix the cooked eggplant, Parmigiano-Reggiano and mozzarella.

c) To make the tomato confit, cut the tomatoes in half lengthwise and scoop out the seeds. On a sheet pan, drizzle some olive oil and place the tomatoes cut-side down with the rosemary, thyme and garlic. Season with sugar, salt and freshly ground black pepper. Bake until they are shriveled and dark red, about 45 minutes.

d) Dust two sheet pans with semolina flour. To make the pasta, roll out the dough until the sheet is just translucent.

e) Cut the rolled-out sheets into 12-inch (30-cm) sections and cover the rest with plastic wrap. Lay the sheets on a dry work surface and using a round 3-inch (7.5-cm) cutter, cut circles into the sheet.

f) Using a piping bag or a spoon, place filling in the middle of the pasta circle, leaving about ¼ inch (6 mm) around the sides. To seal, fold the circle over to create a half-moon shape and use a fork to press along the edges to seal.

g) Use a spritz of water to help seal it if necessary. Carefully place the mezzaluna on the semolina-dusted sheet pans, spaced apart.

h) To make the pesto, in a food processor, add basil, grated Parmigiano-Reggiano, garlic, pignoli nuts, kosher salt and freshly ground black pepper. Slowly pour in the olive oil and process until pureed.

i) Bring a large pot of salted water to a boil. Carefully drop the pasta in the boiling water and cook until al dente, about 2 to 3 minutes.

j) In a sauté pan over low heat, add a drizzle of olive oil and the tomato confit. Add the pasta to the pan and gently shake the pan to mix with the tomatoes.

57. Grown-up tomato-parmesan pasta

SERVES: 2

Ingredients

- 3 tablespoons extra-virgin olive oil
- 1 garlic clove, smashed
- 2 teaspoons chopped fresh rosemary
- Crushed red pepper flakes
- 3 tablespoons tomato paste
- ¾ cup anelli, ditalini, or other short, tubular pasta
- Kosher salt and freshly ground pepper
- ⅓ cup shaved Parmesan cheese
- Fresh basil leaves, for garnish

Directions

a) In a medium saucepan, combine the olive oil and garlic over medium-low heat. Cook, stirring occasionally, until the garlic is fragrant, about 2 minutes. Add the rosemary and a pinch of red pepper flakes and cook until toasted and fragrant, about 1 minute more.

b) Remove the saucepan from the heat. Stir in the tomato paste, then add 2½ cups of water. Return the pan to high heat and bring to a boil. Add the pasta and season generously with salt. Cook, stirring often, until the pasta is al dente, about 12 minutes.

c) Remove the pan from the heat again and stir in the Parmesan. Taste and add more salt and pepper as needed.

d) Divide the pasta between two bowls and top with fresh basil. Serve immediately. Store any leftovers refrigerated in an airtight container for up to 3 days.

58.Pumpkin and sage lasagna with fontina

SERVES: 8 TO 10

Ingredients

- 2 teaspoons extra-virgin olive oil, plus more for greasing
- 1 (14-ounce) can pumpkin puree
- 2 cups whole milk
- 2 teaspoons dried oregano
- 2 teaspoons dried basil
- ¼ teaspoon freshly grated nutmeg
- ¼ teaspoon crushed red pepper flakes
- Kosher salt and freshly ground pepper
- 16 ounces whole-milk ricotta cheese
- 2 garlic cloves, grated
- 1 tablespoon chopped fresh sage leaves, plus 8 whole leaves
- 2 tablespoons chopped fresh parsley
- 1 (12-ounce) box no-boil lasagna noodles
- 1 (12-ounce) jar roasted red peppers, drained and chopped
- 3 cups shredded fontina cheese
- 1 cup grated Parmesan cheese
- 12 to 16 pieces of thinly sliced pepperoni (optional)

Directions

a) Preheat the oven to 375°F. Grease a 9 × 13-inch baking dish.

b) In a medium bowl, whisk together the pumpkin, milk, oregano, basil, nutmeg, red pepper flakes, and a pinch each of salt and pepper. In a separate medium bowl, combine the ricotta, garlic, chopped sage, and parsley and season with salt and pepper.

c) Spread a quarter of the pumpkin sauce (about 1 cup) in the bottom of the prepared baking dish. Add 3 or 4 lasagna sheets, breaking them as needed to fit. It is okay if the sheets do not fully cover the sauce. Layer on half of the ricotta mixture, half of the red peppers, then 1 cup of fontina. Add another quarter of the pumpkin sauce, and place 3 or 4 lasagna noodles on top. Layer on the remaining ricotta mixture, the remaining red peppers, 1 cup of fontina, and then another quarter of the pumpkin sauce. Add the remaining lasagna noodles and the remaining pumpkin sauce. Sprinkle the remaining 1 cup of fontina on top, then the Parmesan cheese. Top with the pepperoni (if using)

d) In a small bowl, toss the whole sage leaves in the 2 teaspoons olive oil. Arrange on top of the lasagna.

e) Cover the lasagna with foil and bake for 45 minutes. Increase the heat to 425°F, remove the foil, and bake until the cheese is bubbling, about 10 minutes more. Let the lasagna stand 10 minutes. Serve. Store any leftovers refrigerated in an airtight container for up to 3 days.

59. Minty Feta and Orzo Salad

SERVES 8

Ingredients

- 1 1/4 C. orzo pasta
- 1 small red onion, diced
- 6 Tablespoons olive oil, divided
- 1/2 C. finely chopped fresh mint leaves
- 3/4 C. dried brown lentils, rinsed
- 1/2 C. chopped fresh dill
- salt and pepper to taste
- 1/3 C. red wine vinegar
- 3 cloves garlic, minced
- 1/2 C. Kalamata olives, pitted and chopped
- 1 1/2 C. crumbled feta cheese

Directions

a) Cook the pasta according to the directions on the package.
b) Bring a salted large saucepan of water to a boil. Cook in it the lentils until it starts boiling.

c) Lower the heat and put it on the lid. Cook the lentils for 22 min. Remove them from the water.

d) Get a small mixing bowl: Combine in it the olive oil, vinegar, and garlic. Whisk them well to make the dressing.

e) Get a large mixing bowl: Toss in it the lentils, dressing, olives, feta cheese, red onion, mint, and dill, with salt and pepper.

f) Wrap a plastic wrap on the salad bowl and place it in the fridge for 2 h 30 min. Adjust the seasoning of the salad then serve it.

60. Fresh Lemon Pasta

SERVES 8

Ingredients

- 1 (16 oz.) package tri-color rotini pasta
- 1 pinch salt and ground black pepper to
- 2 tomatoes, seeded and diced
- taste
- 2 cucumbers - peeled, seeded, and
- 1 avocado, diced
- diced
- 1 squeeze lemon juice
- 1 (4 oz.) can slice black olives
- 1/2 C. Italian dressing, or more to taste
- 1/2 C. shredded Parmesan cheese

Directions

a) Cook the pasta according to the directions on the package.

b) Get a large mixing bowl: Combine in it the pasta, tomatoes, cucumbers, olives, Italian dressing, Parmesan cheese, salt, and pepper. Stir them well.

c) Place the pasta in the fridge for 1 h 15 min.

d) Get a small mixing bowl: Stir in it the lemon juice with avocado. Toss the avocado with pasta salad then serve it.

e) Enjoy.

61. Tortellini Jarred salad

SERVES 2

Ingredients

- 1 (9 oz.) package spinach and cheese
- 1 canning jar tortellini
- salt and ground black pepper to taste
- 1 (4 oz.) jar pesto
- 1/4 C. halved, seeded, and sliced English cucumber
- 1/4 C. halved cherry tomatoes
- 1/4 C. matchstick-sized pieces red onion
- 1/2 C. chopped mache

Directions

a) Cook the pasta according to the directions on the package.

b) Spread the pesto in the jar then top it with the cucumbers, tomatoes, onions, tortellini, and mache. Season them with some salt and pepper.

c) Serve your salad right away or refrigerate it until you are ready to serve it.

62. Romano Linguine Pasta Salad

SERVES 6

Ingredients

- 1 (8 oz.) package linguine pasta
- 1/2 teaspoons red pepper flakes
- 1 (12 oz.) bag broccoli florets, cut into bite size pieces
- 1/4 teaspoons ground black pepper
- salt to taste
- 1/4 C. olive oil
- 4 teaspoons minced garlic
- 1/2 C. finely shredded Romano cheese
- 2 Tablespoons finely chopped fresh flat-leaf parsley

Directions

a) Cook the pasta according to the directions on the package.
b) Bring a pot of water to a boil. Place a steamer on top. Steam in it the broccoli with the lid on for 6 min
c) Place a saucepan over medium heat. Heat the oil in it. Sauté in it the garlic with pepper flakes for 2 min.

d) Get a large mixing bowl: Transfer to it the sautéed garlic mix with pasta, broccoli, Romano cheese, parsley, black pepper, and salt. Mix them well.

e) Adjust the seasoning of the salad. Serve it right away.

f) Enjoy.

63. Vegan Rigatoni Basil

SERVES 6

INGREDIENTS

- 1 1/2 (8 oz.) packages rigatoni pasta
- 6 leaves fresh basil, thinly sliced
- 2 Tablespoons olive oil
- 6 sprigs fresh cilantro, minced
- 2 cloves garlic, minced
- 1/4 C. olive oil
- 1/2 (16 oz.) package tofu, drained and cubed
- 1/2 teaspoons dried thyme
- 1 1/2 teaspoons soy sauce
- 1 small onion, thinly sliced
- 1 large tomato, cubed
- 1 carrot, shredded

Directions

a) Cook the pasta according to the directions on the package.
b) Place a large pan over medium heat. Heat 2 Tablespoons of olive oil in it. Add the garlic and cook it for 1 min 30 sec.

c) Stir in the thyme with tofu. Cook them for 9 min. Stir in the soy sauce and turn off the heat.

d) Get a large mixing bowl: Toss in it the rigatoni, tofu mix, onion, tomato, carrot, basil, and cilantro. Drizzle the olive oil over the pasta salad then serve it.

64. BLT Pasta Salad

Servings Size: 6

Ingredients
- 2 cups elbow macaroni
- 1 ¼ cups mayonnaise
- 2 Tablespoons balsamic vinegar
- 1 cup halved cherry tomatoes
- ¼ cup chopped red bell pepper
- 3 Tablespoons chopped scallions
- ½ cup shredded Cheddar cheese
- Salt and pepper to taste
- ½ teaspoons dill
- 10 bacon slices
- 8 oz. chopped romaine lettuce

Directions
a) Cook the macaroni in a pot of salted water for 10 minutes. Drain and transfer to a salad bowl.
b) Add the mayonnaise, balsamic vinegar, tomatoes, bell pepper, scallions, cheese, salt, pepper, and dill to the macaroni and stir well to combine.
c) Chill for 3 hours.
d) Fry the bacon for 10 minutes, until crispy.
e) Drain the bacon and let cool, then crumble the bacon.
f) Top the salad with the crumbled bacon.
g) Serve on romaine lettuce.

65. Noodle Kugel

Servings Size: 10

Ingredients
- 16 oz. egg noodles
- ¾ cup butter
- 5 beaten eggs
- ¾ cup sugar
- 1 ½ cups applesauce
- ½ cup raisins
- ½ cup chopped pecans
- 1 teaspoons vanilla extract
- 1 Tablespoons cinnamon

Directions
a) Preheat the oven to 350 degrees.
b) Prepare the pasta in a pot of boiling salted water for 5 minutes. Drain.
c) Transfer the egg noodles to a large salad bowl.
d) Stir the butter into the warm/hot noodles until it is melted.
e) Add the remaining ingredients and combine thoroughly.
f) Place the mixture in a 9x13 inch baking dish.
g) Cover with aluminum foil.
h) Bake for 30 minutes.
i) Remove the foil and bake for 15 more minutes.

66. Tortellini Pesto Salad

Servings Size: 6

Ingredients
9 oz. cheese tortellini
¾ cup chopped marinated artichoke hearts
½ cup chopped roasted red pepper
¼ cup sliced Kalamata olives
¼ cup halved cherry tomatoes
3 minced garlic cloves
½ cup mayonnaise
¼ cup prepared basil pesto
2 Tablespoons grated Parmesan cheese
2 Tablespoons olive oil
2 Tablespoons white vinegar

Directions
a) Cook the tortellini in a pot of boiling salted water for 5 minutes.
b) Drain and set aside to cool.
c) Combine the tortellini, marinated artichoke hearts, roasted red pepper, Kalamata olives, halved cherry tomatoes, and garlic in a large bowl.
d) In another bowl, combine the mayonnaise, pesto, parmesan cheese, olive oil, and vinegar.
e) Top the tortellini salad with the dressing and toss to coat.
f) Refrigerate for 1 hour.

67. Confetti Pasta Salad

Servings Size: 6

Ingredients
- 2 cups uncooked multi-colored rotini pasta
- ¾ cup mayonnaise
- ½ package dried Italian dressing
- 1 Tablespoons apple cider vinegar
- Salt and pepper to taste
- 2 minced garlic cloves
- 1 cup chopped tomatoes
- 1 peeled and sliced cucumber
- ½ chopped red bell pepper
- ½ chopped green bell pepper
- ½ cup sliced black olives
- ¼ cup cubed mozzarella cheese

Directions
a) Cook the pasta in a pot of salted boiling water for 10 minutes. Drain.
b) Combine the mayonnaise, dry Italian salad dressing, vinegar, salt, pepper, and garlic in a small bowl.
c) Using a large salad bowl, add the cooked pasta and remaining ingredients and toss with the dressing.
d) Refrigerate for 1 hour.

68. Caprese Pasta Salad

Servings: 8

Ingredients:

- 2 cups cooked penne pasta
- 1 cup pesto
- 2 chopped tomatoes
- 1 cup diced mozzarella cheese
- Salt and pepper to taste
- 1/8 teaspoons oregano
- 2 teaspoons red wine vinegar

Directions:

a) Cook the pasta according to the package directions, which should take around 12 minutes. Drain.

b) In a large mixing bowl, combine the pasta, pesto, tomatoes, and cheese; season with salt, pepper, and oregano.

c) Drizzle red wine vinegar on top.

d) Set aside for 1 hour in the refrigerator.

69. Mozzarella fritters and spaghetti

Ingredient

- 2 Garlic cloves
- 1 bunch fresh parsley
- 3 Salad onions; thinly sliced
- 225 grams Lean minced pork
- 2 tablespoons Freshly grated Parmesan
- 1 tablespoon Olive oil
- 150 grams Spaghetti or tagliatelle
- 100 milliliters stock
- 400 grams can chopped tomatoes
- 1 pinch Sugar and 1 dash Soy sauce
- Salt and pepper
- 1 Egg
- 1 tablespoon Olive oil
- 75 milliliters Milk
- 50 grams' Plain flour
- 150 grams Smoked mozzarella
- Sunflower oil; for frying
- 1 Lemon

Directions:

a) Crush the garlic and finely chop the parsley. Mix together the mince, salad onions, garlic, Parmesan, parsley and plenty of salt and pepper.

b) Shape into eight firm balls.

c) Cook the meatballs until well browned. Pour in the stock.

d) Cook the pasta in a large pan of boiling salted water.

70. One-pot creamed corn bucatini

SERVES: 6

Ingredients

- 4 tablespoons salted butter
- 4 ears yellow corn, kernels sliced from the cob
- 2 garlic cloves, minced or grated
- 2 tablespoons fresh thyme leaves
- 1 jalapeño or red Fresno pepper, seeded and thinly sliced
- 2 green onions, chopped
- Kosher salt and freshly ground pepper
- 1 (1-pound box) bucatini
- $\frac{1}{2}$ cup grated Parmesan cheese
- 2 tablespoons crème fraîche
- $\frac{1}{4}$ cup fresh basil leaves, roughly torn

Directions

a) Melt the butter in a large Dutch oven over medium heat. Add the corn, garlic, thyme, jalapeño, green onions, and a pinch each of salt and pepper. Cook, stirring occasionally, until the corn is golden and caramelizing on the edges, about 5 minutes.

b) Add $4\frac{1}{2}$ cups of water, increase the heat to high, and bring to a boil. Add the pasta and season with salt. Cook, stirring often, until most of the liquid has been absorbed and the pasta is al dente, about 10 minutes.

c) Remove the pot from the heat and stir in the Parmesan, crème fraîche, and basil. If the sauce feels too thick, add a splash of water to thin it out. Serve immediately.

71. Spinach and artichoke mac-and-cheese

SERVES: 6 TO 8

Ingredients

- 6 tablespoons salted butter, at room temperature, plus more for greasing
- 1 (1-pound) box short-cut pasta, such as macaroni
- 2 cups whole milk
- 1 (8-ounce) package cream cheese, cubed
- 3 cups shredded sharp cheddar cheese
- Kosher salt and freshly ground pepper
- Ground cayenne pepper
- 2 cups packed fresh baby spinach, chopped
- 1 (8-ounce) jar marinated artichokes, drained and roughly chopped
- $1\frac{1}{2}$ cups crushed Ritz crackers (about 1 sleeve)
- $\frac{3}{4}$ teaspoon garlic powder

Directions

a) Preheat the oven to 375°F. Grease a 9 × 13-inch baking dish.

b) In a large saucepan, bring 4 cups of salted water to a boil over high heat. Add the pasta and cook, stirring occasionally, for 8 minutes. Stir in the milk and cream cheese and cook until the cream cheese has melted and the pasta is al dente, about 5 minutes more.

c) Remove the pan from the heat and stir in 2 cups of the cheddar and 3 tablespoons of the butter. Season with salt, pepper, and cayenne. Stir in the spinach and artichokes. If the sauce feels too thick, add $\frac{1}{4}$ cup of milk or water to thin it.

d) Transfer the mixture to the prepared baking dish. Top with the remaining 1 cup of cheddar.

e) In a medium bowl, stir together the crackers, the remaining 3 tablespoons of butter, and the garlic powder. Sprinkle the crumbs evenly over the mac and cheese.

f) Bake until the sauce is bubbling and the crumbs are golden, about 20 minutes. Let cool for 5 minutes and serve. Store any leftovers refrigerated in an airtight container for up to 3 days.

72. Decadent Spinach-Stuffed Shells

Ingredients

- 1 package (12 ounces) jumbo pasta shells
- 1 jar (24 ounces) roasted red pepper and garlic pasta sauce
- 2 packages (8 ounces each) cream cheese, softened
- 1 cup roasted garlic Alfredo sauce
- Dash salt
- Dash pepper
- Dash crushed red pepper flakes, optional
- 2 cups shredded Italian cheese blend
- 1/2 cup grated Parmesan cheese
- 1 package (10 ounces) frozen chopped spinach, thawed and squeezed dry
- 1/2 cup finely chopped water-packed artichoke hearts
- 1/4 cup finely chopped roasted sweet red pepper
- Additional Parmesan cheese, optional

Directions

a) Preheat oven to 350°. Cook pasta shells according to package directions for al dente. Drain.

b) Spread 1 cup sauce into a greased 13x9-in. baking dish. In a large bowl, beat cream cheese, Alfredo sauce and seasonings until blended. Stir in cheeses and vegetables. Spoon into shells. Arrange in prepared baking dish.

c) Pour remaining sauce over top. Bake, covered, 20 minutes. If desired, sprinkle with additional Parmesan cheese. Bake, uncovered, 10-15 minutes longer or until cheese is melted.

73. Butternut and Chard Pasta Bake

Ingredient

- 3 cups uncooked bow tie pasta
- 2 cups fat-free ricotta cheese
- 4 large eggs
- 3 cups frozen cubed butternut squash, thawed and divided
- 1 teaspoon dried thyme
- 1/2 teaspoon salt, divided
- 1/4 teaspoon ground nutmeg
- 1 cup coarsely chopped shallots
- 1-1/2 cups chopped Swiss chard, stems removed
- 2 tablespoons olive oil
- 1-1/2 cups panko bread crumbs
- 1/3 cup coarsely chopped fresh parsley
- 1/4 teaspoon garlic powder

Directions

a) Preheat oven to 375°. Cook pasta according to package directions for al dente; drain. Meanwhile, place the ricotta, eggs, 1-1/2 cups squash, thyme, 1/4 teaspoon salt and nutmeg in a food processor; process until smooth. Pour into a large bowl.

b) Stir in pasta, shallots, Swiss chard and remaining squash. Transfer to a greased 13x9-in. baking dish.

c) In a large skillet, heat oil over medium-high heat. Add bread crumbs; cook and stir until golden brown, 2-3 minutes. Stir in parsley, garlic powder and remaining 1/4 teaspoon salt. Sprinkle over pasta mixture.

d) Bake, uncovered, until set and topping is golden brown, 30-35 minutes.

SAUSAGE PASTA

74. Southwestern Lasagna

Servings Size: 6

Ingredients
- 2 Tablespoons olive oil
- 1 chopped onion
- 1 ½ cups shredded Cheddar cheese
- 1 Tablespoons chopped jalapeno pepper
- 4 minced garlic cloves
- 3 cups hot sausage meat
- ½ cup picante sauce
- 1 teaspoons Italian seasoning or to taste
- 4 cups tomato sauce
- 2 cups shredded Pepper Jack cheese
- 15 corn tortillas

Directions
a) Preheat your oven to 350 degrees F.
b) Heat the olive oil in a large skillet.
c) Sauté the garlic, jalapeno pepper, and onion for 5 minutes.
d) Add the sausage meat and season with the Italian seasoning.
e) Stir in the tomato sauce and picante sauce.
f) Combine all ingredients well.
g) Cover the skillet and simmer for 15 minutes.
h) Coat a 9x13 baking dish with non-stick spray.
i) Layer the baking dish with 1 tortilla, a layer of sausage and sauce, and a layer of pepper jack cheese.
j) Create 2 more layers.
k) Top the third layer with the cheddar cheese.
l) Bake for 45 minutes.

75. Romano Rigatoni Casserole

SERVES 6

Ingredients

- 1 lb. ground sausage
- 1/4 C. Romano cheese, grated
- 1 (28 oz.) can Italian-style tomato sauce
- chopped parsley, to garnish
- 1 (14 1/2 oz.) can cannellini beans, drained and rinsed
- 1 (16 oz.) BOX rigatoni pasta
- 1/2 teaspoons minced garlic
- 1 teaspoons Italian seasoning
- 3 C. shredded mozzarella cheese

Directions

a) Before you do anything set the oven to 350 F. Grease a large casserole dish with some butter or oil.

b) Place a large pot on medium heat. Add the garlic with sausages and cook them for 6 min.

c) Add the tomato sauce, beans, and Italian seasoning then cook them for 5 min on low heat.

d) Cook the pasta according to the manufacturer's directions. Drain the pasta and sit it into the pot.

e) Pour half of the sausage pasta mix in the greased casserole then top it with half of the mozzarella cheese. Repeat the process to make another layer.

f) Top the casserole with romano cheese then put on it a piece of foil. Cook the rigatoni casserole in the oven for 26 min.

g) Serve your rigatoni warm.

76. Cheesy Pepperoni Rotini Salad

SERVES 8

Ingredients

- 1 (16 oz.) package tri-color rotini pasta
- 1 (8 oz.) package mozzarella cheese
- 1/4 lb. sliced pepperoni sausage
- 1 C. fresh broccoli florets
- 1 (16 oz.) bottle Italian-style salad
- 1 (6 oz.) can black olives, drained
- dressing

Directions

a) Cook the pasta according to the directions on the package.

b) Get a large mixing bowl: Toss in it the pasta, pepperoni, broccoli, olives, cheese, and dressing.

c) Adjust the seasoning of the salad and place it in the fridge for 1 h 10 min. Serve it.

77. Roman Fun Pasta

SERVES 6

Ingredients

- 1 (12 oz.) package bow tie pasta
- 1 (28 oz.) can Italian-style plum tomatoes, drained
- 2 Tablespoons olive oil
- 1 lb. sweet Italian sausage, crumbled
- 1 1/2 C. heavy cream
- 1/2 teaspoons salt
- 1/2 teaspoons red pepper flakes
- 3 Tablespoons minced fresh parsley
- 1/2 C. diced onion
- 3 cloves garlic, minced

Directions

a) Boil your pasta in water and salt for 9 minutes then remove the liquids.
b) Begin to stir fry your pepper flakes and sausage in oil until it the meat is browned then add the garlic and onions.
c) Let the onions cook until they are soft then add in the salt, cream, and tomatoes.

d) Stir the mix then get everything gently boiling.

e) Let the mix gently cook with a low level of heat for 9 minutes then add in the pasta.

f) Stir the mix, to evenly cook the noodles, then coat everything with parsley.

78. Tortellini Classico

SERVES 8

Ingredients

- 1 lb. sweet Italian sausage, casings removed
- 1/2 teaspoons dried oregano
- 1 C. diced onion
- 1 (8 oz.) can tomato sauce
- 2 cloves garlic, minced
- 1 1/2 C. sliced zucchini
- 5 C. broth
- 8 oz. fresh tortellini pasta
- 1/2 C. water
- 3 Tablespoons diced fresh parsley
- 1/2 C. red wine
- 4 large tomatoes - peeled, seeded and diced
- 1 C. thinly sliced carrots
- 1/2 Tablespoons packed fresh basil leaves

Directions

a) In a large pot brown your sausage all over.

b) Then remove the meat from the pan.

c) Begin to stir fry your garlic and onions in the drippings then add-in: the sausage, broth, tomato sauce, water, oregano, wine, basil, tomatoes, and carrots.

d) Get the mix boiling, set the heat to low, and let everything cook for 35 Minutes.

e) Remove any fat which rises to the top then add in the parsley and zucchini.

f) Continue cooking the mix for 20 more minutes before adding in the pasta and letting everything cooking 15 more minutes.

79. Spanish Lasagna

SERVES 12

Ingredients

- 4 C. canned minced tomatoes
- 1 (32 oz.) container ricotta cheese
- 1 (7 oz.) can dice green chiles
- 4 eggs, lightly beaten
- 1 (4 oz.) can dice jalapeno peppers
- 1 (16 oz.) package Mexican style shredded four cheese blend
- 1 onion, diced
- 3 cloves garlic, minced
- 1 (8 oz.) package no-cook lasagna noodles
- 10 sprigs fresh cilantro, chopped
- 2 Tablespoons ground cumin
- 2 lbs. chorizo sausage

Directions

a) Boil the following for 2 minutes, then simmer on low for 55 Minutes: cilantro, tomatoes, cumin, green chilies, garlic, onion, and jalapenos.

b) Get a bowl, mix beaten eggs, and ricotta.

c) Set your oven to 350 degrees before continuing.

d) Stir-fry your chorizos. Then remove oil excess and crumble the meat.

e) In your baking dish, apply a light covering of sauce then layer: sausage, 1/2 of your sauce, 1/2 shredded cheese, lasagna noodles, ricotta, more noodles, all remaining sauce, and more shredded cheese.

f) Coat some foil with nonstick spray, and cover the lasagna. Cook for 30 minutes covered, and 15 minutes without cover.

80. Ziti with Sausage

Servings: 8

Ingredients:

- 1 lb. crumbled Italian sausage
- 1 cup sliced mushrooms
- ½ cup diced celery
- 1 diced onion
- 3 minced garlic cloves
- 42 oz. store-bought spaghetti sauce or homemade
- Salt and pepper to taste
- ½ teaspoon oregano
- ½ teaspoon basil
- 1 lb. uncooked ziti pasta
- 1 cup shredded mozzarella cheese
- ½ cup grated parmesan cheese
- 3 Tablespoon chopped parsley

Directions:

a) In a skillet, brown the sausage, mushrooms, onion, and celery for 5 minutes.

b) After that, add the garlic. Cook for another 3 minutes. Remove from the equation.

c) Add the spaghetti sauce, salt, pepper, oregano, and basil to a separate skillet.

d) Simmer the sauce for 15 minutes.

e) Prepare the pasta in a pan according to the package directions while the sauce cooks. Drain.

f) Preheat oven to 350 degrees Fahrenheit.

g) In a baking dish, put ziti, sausage mixture, and shredded mozzarella in two layers.

h) Sprinkle parsley and parmesan cheese over the top.

i) Preheat oven to 350°F and bake for 25 minutes.

81. Saucy Lasagna

Servings: 4

Ingredients:

- 1 ½ lb. crumbled spicy Italian sausage
- 5 cups store-bought spaghetti sauce
- 1 cup tomato sauce
- 1 teaspoon Italian seasoning
- ½ cup red wine
- 1 Tablespoon sugar
- 1 Tablespoon oil
- 5 minced garlic gloves
- 1 diced onion
- 1 cup shredded mozzarella cheese
- 1 cup shredded provolone cheese
- 2 cups ricotta cheese
- 1 cup cottage cheese
- 2 large eggs
- ¼ cup milk
- 9 noodles lasagna noodles – parboiled
- ¼ cup grated parmesan cheese

Directions:

a) Preheat oven to 375 degrees Fahrenheit.

b) In a skillet, brown the crumbled sausage for 5 minutes. Any grease should be discarded.

c) In a large pot, combine the pasta sauce, tomato sauce, Italian seasoning, red wine, and sugar and mix thoroughly.

d) In a skillet, heat the olive oil. Then, for 5 minutes, sauté the garlic and onion.

e) Incorporate the sausage, garlic, and onion into the sauce.

f) After that, cover the saucepan and leave it to simmer for 45 minutes.

g) In a mixing dish, combine the mozzarella and provolone cheeses.

h) In a separate bowl, combine the ricotta, cottage cheese, eggs, and milk.

i) In a 9 x 13 baking dish, pour 12 cup of sauce into the bottom of the dish.

j) Now arrange the noodles, sauce, ricotta, and mozzarella in the baking dish in three layers.

k) Spread parmesan cheese over the top.

l) Bake in a covered dish for 30 minutes.

m) Bake for another 15 minutes after uncovering the dish.

82. Slow Cooker Lasagna

Servings Size: 8

Ingredients
- 1 lb. ground beef
- ½ lb. crumbled Italian spicy sausage meat
- 1 chopped onion
- 3 minced garlic cloves
- 1 cup sliced mushrooms
- 3 cups tomato sauce – homemade is good, and jarred is fine
- 1 cup water
- 8 oz. tomato paste
- 1 teaspoons Italian seasoning
- 12 oz. oven-ready lasagna noodles (not the regular kind)
- 1 ¼ cups ricotta cheese
- ½ cup grated Parmesan cheese
- 2 cups shredded mozzarella cheese
- 1 additional cup shredded mozzarella cheese

Directions
a) Brown the beef, sausage, onion, garlic, and mushrooms in a large skillet for 5 minutes.
b) Drain any fat.
c) Stir in the sauce, water, tomato paste, Italian seasoning, and combine well.
d) Simmer for 5 minutes.
e) Combine the ricotta, parmesan, and 2 cups of mozzarella cheese in a bowl.
f) Create layers (2 to 3) of meat, sauce, double layer of noodles (break them in half), and cheese mixture.
g) Top with 1 cup of shredded mozzarella cheese.
h) Cook for 4 hours on low.

83. Penne and Smoked Sausage

Ingredient

- 2 cups uncooked penne pasta
- 1 pound smoked sausage, cut into 1/4-inch slices
- 1-1/2 cups 2% milk
- 1 can (10-3/4 ounces) condensed cream of celery soup, undiluted
- 1-1/2 cups cheddar french-fried onions, divided
- 1 cup shredded part-skim mozzarella cheese, divided
- 1 cup frozen peas

Directions

a) Preheat oven to 375°. Cook pasta according to package directions.

b) Meanwhile, in a large skillet, brown sausage over medium heat 5 minutes; drain. In a large bowl, combine milk and soup. Stir in 1/2 cup onions, 1/2 cup cheese, peas and sausage. Drain pasta; stir into sausage mixture.

c) Transfer to a greased 13x9-in. baking dish. Cover and bake until bubbly, 25-30 minutes. Sprinkle with remaining onions and cheese. Bake, uncovered, until cheese is melted, 3-5 minutes longer.

d) Freeze option: Sprinkle remaining onions and cheese over unbaked casserole. Cover and freeze. To use, partially thaw in refrigerator overnight. Remove from refrigerator 30 minutes before baking. Preheat oven to 375°. Bake casserole as directed, increasing time as necessary to heat through and for a thermometer inserted in center to read 165°.

84. Spinach and three-cheese stuffed shells

SERVES: 6 TO 8

Ingredients

- 2 tablespoons extra-virgin olive oil
- 1 pound ground spicy Italian sausage
- 2 (28-ounce) cans crushed tomatoes, such as San Marzano or Pomi tomatoes
- 1 red bell pepper, seeded and sliced
- 2 teaspoons dried oregano
- $\frac{1}{2}$ teaspoon crushed red pepper flakes, plus more as needed
- Kosher salt and freshly ground pepper
- 1 (8-ounce) bag frozen chopped spinach, thawed and squeezed dry
- 1 (1-pound) box jumbo pasta shells
- 16 ounces whole-milk ricotta cheese
- 2 cups shredded Gouda cheese
- 1 cup fresh basil leaves, chopped, plus more for serving
- 8 ounces' fresh mozzarella cheese, torn

Directions

a) Preheat the oven to 350°F.

b) Heat the olive oil in a large oven-safe skillet over medium-high heat. When the oil shimmers, add the sausage and cook, breaking it up with a wooden spoon, until browned, 5 to 8 minutes. Reduce the heat to low and add the crushed tomatoes, bell pepper, oregano, red pepper flakes, and a pinch each of salt and pepper. Simmer until the sauce thickens slightly, 10 to 15 minutes. Stir in the spinach. Taste and add more salt, pepper, and red pepper flakes.

c) Meanwhile, bring a large saucepan of salted water to a boil over high heat. Add the shells and cook according to the package directions, until al dente. Drain well.

d) In a medium bowl, combine the ricotta, Gouda, and basil. Transfer the mix to a gallon-size zip-top bag. Push the mixture into one corner of the bag, squeeze the air out of the top of the bag, and snip about $\frac{1}{2}$ inch off that corner.

e) Working with one at a time, pipe about 1 tablespoon of the cheese mixture into each shell, then place them in the skillet. Sprinkle the shells evenly with mozzarella.

f) Transfer the skillet to the oven and bake until the cheese has melted and is lightly browning on top, 25 to 30 minutes.

85. Classical Lasagna II

SERVES 12

Ingredients

- 1 lb. sweet Italian sausage
- 1 Tablespoons salt
- 3/4 lb. lean ground beef
- 1/4 teaspoons ground black pepper
- 1/2 C. minced onion
- 4 Tablespoons diced fresh parsley
- 2 cloves garlic, crushed
- 12 lasagna noodles
- 1 (28 oz.) can crushed tomatoes
- 16 oz. ricotta cheese
- 2 (6 oz.) cans tomato paste
- 1 egg
- 2 (6.5 oz.) cans canned tomato sauce
- 1/2 teaspoons salt
- 1/2 C. water
- 3/4 lb. mozzarella cheese, sliced
- 2 Tablespoons white sugar

- 3/4 C. grated Parmesan cheese
- 1 1/2 teaspoons dried basil leaves
- 1/2 teaspoons fennel seeds
- 1 teaspoons Italian seasoning

Directions

a) Stir fry your garlic, sausage, onion, and beef until the meat is fully done. Then add in 2

b) Tablespoons parsley, crushed tomatoes, pepper, tomato paste, 1 Tablespoons salt, tomato sauce, Italian spice, water, fennel seeds, sugar, and basil.

c) Get the mix boiling, set the heat to low, and let the contents gently cook for 90 Minutes. Stir the mix at least 4 times.

d) Now get your pasta boiling in water and salt for 9 minutes then remove the liquids.

e) Get a bowl, combine 1/2 teaspoons salt, ricotta, the rest of the parsley, and the eggs.

f) Set your oven to 375 degrees before doing anything else.

g) Coat the bottom of a casserole dish with 1.5 C. of the meat and tomato mix then place six pieces of lasagna on top.

h) Add half of the cheese mixture then 1/3 of the mozzarella.

i) Add 1.5 C. of tomato meat mix again and a quarter of a C. of parmesan.

j) Continue layering in this manner until all the ingredients have been used up.

k) Try to end with mozzarella and parmesan.

l) Take a large piece of foil and coat it with nonstick spray then cover the casserole dish with the foil and cook everything in the oven for 30 Minutes.

m) Now take off the foil and continue cooking the lasagna for 20 more Minutes.

n) Serve the dish after letting everything rest for at least 30 minutes (longer is better).

86. Pepperoni Lasagna

SERVES 12

Ingredients

- 3/4 lb. ground beef
- 1/4 teaspoons ground black pepper
- 1/2 lb. salami, chopped
- 9 lasagna noodles
- 1/2 lb. pepperoni sausage, chopped
- 4 C. shredded mozzarella cheese
- 1 onion, minced
- 2 C. cottage cheese
- 2 (14.5 oz.) cans stewed tomatoes
- 9 slices white American cheese
- 16 oz. tomato sauce
- grated Parmesan cheese
- 6 oz. tomato paste
- 1 teaspoons garlic powder
- 1 teaspoons dried oregano
- 1/2 teaspoons salt

Directions

a) Fry your pepperoni, beef, onions, and salami for 10 Minutes. Remove oil excess. Enter everything into your slow cooker on low with some pepper, tomato sauce and paste, salt, stewed tomatoes, oregano, and garlic powder for 2 hours.

b) Turn on your oven to 350 degrees before continuing.

c) Boil your lasagna in saltwater until al dente for 10 minutes, then remove all water.

d) In your baking dish, apply a light covering of sauce then layer: 1/3 noodles, 1 1/4 C. mozzarella, 2/3 C. cottage cheese, American cheese slices, 4 Tablespoons parmesan, 1/3 meat. Continue until the dish is full.

e) Cook for 30 Minutes.

CLASSIC PASTA

87. Ramen Noodle Salad

Servings Size: 6

Ingredients
- 6 oz. of crushed ramen noodles
- 1 cup slivered almonds
- 1 Tablespoons sesame seeds
- ¼ canola oil
- 3 Tablespoons white vinegar
- 1 ramen noodle flavor packet
- ½ cup white sugar
- 2 Tablespoons soy sauce
- 2 cups package slaw mix
- ½ cup chopped water chestnuts
- 4 chopped scallions
- Salt and pepper to taste

Directions
a) Place the ramen noodles, slivered almonds, and sesame seeds on a baking sheet and bake for 10 minutes at 350 degrees. Let cool.
b) Combine the oil, vinegar, sugar, ramen flavor packet, and vinegar in a small pan and boil for 1 minute.
c) Stir in the soy sauce.
d) Transfer the slaw mix, water chestnuts, and scallion to a salad bowl.
e) Stir in the noodle mixture and oil and vinegar mixture and toss well.
f) Season with salt and pepper, if needed.

88. Angel Hair Carbonara

Servings Size: 2

Ingredients
- 4 slices of bacon
- $\frac{1}{2}$ lb. angel hair pasta
- $\frac{1}{4}$ cup plain sour cream
- $\frac{1}{4}$ cup heavy cream
- $\frac{1}{4}$ cup grated Pecorino Romano
- 1 egg
- $\frac{1}{4}$ teaspoons Italian seasoning
- $\frac{1}{4}$ teaspoons red pepper flakes
- $\frac{1}{2}$ teaspoons garlic salt

Directions
a) Fry the bacon in a skill for 7 minutes.
b) Drain, let cool, and crumble.
c) Cook the angel hair in a pot of salted water for 5 minutes. Drain.
d) Combine the yogurt, sour cream, Pecorino Romano, egg, and all seasonings in a bowl.
e) Toss the pasta with the cheese mixture and top with the crumbled bacon.

89. Penne with Vodka Sauce

Servings Size: 4

Ingredients
- 16 oz. penne pasta
- 1 Tablespoons olive oil
- 1 diced onion
- 3 minced garlic cloves
- ¼ lb. chopped prosciutto
- 28 oz. canned crushed tomatoes
- 1 cup tomato sauce
- ½ cup vodka
- 1 cup heavy cream
- 1 cup Parmesan cheese
- ½ cup chopped fresh basil leaves
- ¼ teaspoons thyme
- 1 Tablespoons chopped parsley
- Salt to taste
- 1 teaspoons sugar

Directions
a) Cook the pasta in a pot of salted water for 10 minutes. Drain.
b) Heat the oil in a large skillet or another pot.
c) Sauté the onion, garlic, prosciutto for 2 minutes.
d) Add the crushed tomatoes and tomato sauce.
e) Stir and simmer for 5 minutes.
f) Add the vodka and heavy cream and simmer for 20 minutes.
g) Season with basil, thyme, parsley, salt, and sugar.
h) Taste and adjust seasoning.
i) Stir in the cooked pasta and parmesan cheese and simmer for 5 minutes.

90. Penne alla vodka

SERVES: 8

Ingredients

- 4 tablespoons salted butter
- 2 garlic cloves, minced or grated
- $\frac{1}{2}$ teaspoon crushed red pepper flakes
- $\frac{1}{2}$ cup vodka
- 1 (28-ounce) can crushed tomatoes, such as San Marzano or Pomi tomatoes
- $\frac{1}{2}$ cup sun-dried tomatoes packed in olive oil, drained and chopped
- Kosher salt and freshly ground pepper
- $\frac{3}{4}$ cup heavy cream
- 1 (1-pound) box penne
- 1 cup grated Parmesan cheese, plus more for serving
- Fresh basil, for serving

Directions

a) In a large saucepan, combine the butter, garlic, and red pepper flakes over medium-low heat. Cook, stirring often, until the butter is melted and the garlic is fragrant, about 5 minutes. Add the vodka and bring to a simmer. Cook until reduced by one-third, 2 to 3 minutes more. Add the crushed tomatoes, sun-dried tomatoes, and a large pinch each of salt and pepper. Simmer the sauce over medium heat until reduced slightly, 10 to 15 minutes. Transfer the sauce to a blender or use an immersion blender to puree the sauce until smooth, 1 minute. Stir in the cream until combined.

b) Meanwhile, bring a large saucepan of salted water to a boil over high heat. Add the penne and cook according to the package directions, until al dente. Drain and add the pasta and Parmesan to the sauce, tossing to combine.

c) To serve traditionally, divide the pasta among eight plates or bowls. Garnish with basil and Parmesan.

91. Lemon basil pasta with brussels sprouts

SERVES: 8

Ingredients

- 1 (1-pound) box long-cut pasta, such as bucatini or fettuccine
- 4 ounces thinly sliced prosciutto, torn
- 3 tablespoons extra-virgin olive oil
- 1 pound Brussels sprouts, halved or quartered if large
- Kosher salt and freshly ground pepper
- 2 tablespoons balsamic vinegar
- 1 jalapeño pepper, seeded and chopped
- 1 tablespoon fresh thyme leaves
- 1 cup Lemon Basil Pesto
- 4 ounces' goat cheese, crumbled
- ⅓ cup grated Manchego cheese
- Zest and juice of 1 lemon

Directions

a) Preheat the oven to 375°F.

b) Bring a large pot of salted water to a boil over high heat. Add the pasta and cook according to the package directions until al dente. Reserve 1 cup of the pasta cooking water, then drain.

c) Meanwhile, arrange the prosciutto in an even layer on a parchment paper-lined baking sheet. Bake until crispy, 8 to 10 minutes.

d) While the pasta cooks and the prosciutto bakes, heat the olive oil in a large skillet over medium heat. When the oil shimmers, add the Brussels sprouts and cook, stirring occasionally, until golden brown, 8 to 10 minutes. Season with salt and pepper. Reduce the heat to medium-low and add the vinegar, jalapeño, and thyme and cook until the sprouts are glazed, 1 to 2 minutes more.

e) Remove the skillet from the heat and add the drained pasta, the pesto, goat cheese, Manchego, lemon zest, and lemon juice. Add about $\frac{1}{4}$ cup of the pasta cooking water and stir to create a sauce.

f) Add 1 tablespoon more at a time until your desired consistency is reached. Taste and add more salt and pepper as needed.

g) Divide the pasta evenly among eight bowls or plates and top each with crispy prosciutto.

92. Crimini Pasta Bake

SERVES 6

Ingredients

- 8 crimini mushrooms
- 1/3 C. parmesan cheese, grated
- 1 C. broccoli floret
- 3 Tablespoons herbs de Provence
- 1 C. spinach, fresh leaf, tightly packed
- 2 Tablespoons extra virgin olive oil
- 2 red bell peppers, julienned
- 1 Tablespoons salt
- 1 large onion, chopped
- 1/2 Tablespoons pepper
- 1 C. mozzarella cheese, shredded
- 1 C. tomato sauce
- 2/3 lb. pasta (fettuccine or penne works well)

Directions

a) Before you do anything set the oven to 450 F. Grease a casserole dish with oil or cooking spray.

b) Get a large mixing bowl: Toss the mushrooms, broccoli, spinach, pepper, and onion in it.

c) Add 1 Tablespoons of olive oil, salt, pepper and toss them again.

d) Spread the veggies in the greased dish and cook it in the oven for 10 min.

e) Cook the pasta until it becomes dente. Drain the pasta and set it aside.

f) Get a large mixing bowl: Mix 1 Tablespoons of olive oil with baked veggies, pasta, herbs, and mozzarella cheese. Spread the mix back in the casserole dish.

g) Sprinkle the cheese on top then cook it for 20 min. Serve it warm and enjoy.

93. Sunny Hot Spaghetti

SERVES 2

Ingredients

- 2 1/2 C. cooked spaghetti
- 1 teaspoons oregano
- 1/4 C. olive oil
- 2 Tablespoons fresh garlic
- 8 pepperoncini peppers, finely minced
- 1/2 C. spaghetti sauce

Directions

a) Place a large pan on medium heat. Heat the oil in it. Add the herbs with peppers and cook them for 4 min.

b) Stir in the sauce with cooked spaghetti then cook it for 3 min.

c) Serve your spaghetti warm right away.

94. Puttanesca

SERVES 4

Ingredients

- 8 oz. pasta
- 2 Tablespoons tomato paste
- 1/2 C. olive oil
- 3 Tablespoons capers
- 3 cloves garlic, minced
- 20 Greek olives, pitted and coarsely diced
- 2 C. diced tomatoes
- 1/2 teaspoons crushed red pepper flakes
- 4 anchovy filets, rinsed and diced

Directions

a) Boil your pasta in water and salt for 9 Minutes then remove all the liquids.

b) Now being to stir fry your garlic in oil until it is browned all over.

c) Then add the tomatoes and cook the mix for 7 minutes before adding in: the pepper flakes, anchovies, olives, tomato paste, and capers.

d) Let the mix cook for 12 Minutes and stir everything at least 2 times.

e) Now add in the pasta and stir everything to evenly coat the noodles.

95. Parmesan Orzo

SERVES 6

Ingredients

- 1/2 C. butter, divided
- garlic powder to taste
- 8 pearl onions
- salt and pepper to taste
- 1 C. uncooked orzo pasta
- 1/2 C. grated Parmesan cheese
- 1/2 C. sliced fresh mushrooms
- 1/4 C. fresh parsley
- 1 C. water
- 1/2 C. white wine

Directions

a) Stir fry your onions in half of the butter until it is browned then add in the rest of the butter, mushrooms, and the orzo.

b) Continue frying everything for 7 Minutes.

c) Now combine in the wine and the water and get everything boiling.

d) Once the mix is boiling, set the heat to low, and cook everything for 9 Minutes after adding in the pepper, salt and garlic powder.

e) Once the orzo is done top it with parsley and parmesan.

96. Pasta Rustica

PREP TIME: 10 Minutes

COOKING TIME: 35 Minutes

SERVES 4

Ingredients

- 1 lb. farfalle (bow tie) pasta
- 1 (8 oz.) package mushrooms, sliced
- 1/3 C. olive oil
- 1 Tablespoons dried oregano
- 1 clove garlic, chopped
- 1 Tablespoons paprika
- 1/4 C. butter
- salt and pepper to taste
- 2 small zucchinis, quartered and sliced
- 1 onion, chopped
- 1 tomato, chopped

Directions

a) Boil your pasta for 10 minutes in water and salt. Remove excess liquid and set aside.

b) Fry your salt, pepper, garlic, paprika, zucchini, oregano, mushrooms, onion, and tomato, for 17 minutes in olive oil.

c) Mix the veggies and pasta.

97. Egg noodle in Germany

SERVES 6

Ingredients

- kosher salt
- 3 Tablespoons flat-leaf parsley, chopped
- 1 (12 oz.) packages wide egg noodles
- fresh ground black pepper
- 4-6 Tablespoons cold unsalted butter, cut into bits

Directions

a) In a large pan of lightly salted boiling water, cook the egg noodles for about 5 minutes, stirring occasionally.

b) Drain well, reserving 1/4 C. of the cooking liquid.

c) In a medium skillet, add the reserved hot cooking liquid on low heat.

d) Slowly, add the butter, beating continuously till a creamy sauce forms.

e) Stir in the parsley, salt, and black pepper.

f) Add the noodles and toss to coat well.

g) Serve immediately.

98. Italian Noodles with Croutons

SERVES 4

Ingredients

- 12 oz. egg noodles
- 1 pinch salt
- 1/2 C. unsalted butter
- 1/4 teaspoons pepper
- 2 slices white bread, torn

Directions

a) In a large pan of boiling water, prepare the egg noodles according to the package's directions.

b) Meanwhile for croutons in a small frying pan, melt the butter on medium heat and cook the bread pieces till lightly crispy.

c) Stir in the salt and black pepper and remove everything from the heat.

d) In a serving bowl, mix the noodles and croutons and serve

99. Loaded Pasta Shells Lasagna

Ingredient

- 4 cups shredded mozzarella cheese
- 1 carton (15 ounces) ricotta cheese
- 1 package (10 ounces) frozen chopped spinach, thawed and squeezed dry
- 1 package (12 ounces) jumbo pasta shells, cooked and drained
- 3-1/2 cups spaghetti sauce
- Grated Parmesan cheese, optional

Directions

a) Preheat oven to 350°. Combine cheeses and spinach; stuff into shells. Arrange in a greased 13x9-in. baking dish. Pour spaghetti sauce over the shells. Cover and bake until heated through, about 30 minutes.

b) If desired, sprinkle with Parmesan cheese after baking.

100. Scuola di Pasta

Directions

d) To roll the pasta dough, adjust a pasta sheeter gauge to the thickest setting.

e) Dust a baking sheet with semolina.

f) Remove the pasta dough from the refrigerator and cut it into quarters.

g) Dust one segment of the dough lightly with flour and pass it through the pasta sheeter, dusting the dough with flour again as it passes through the sheeter, to create long sheets.

h) Adjust the sheeter to the next thinnest setting and pass the dough through again. Continue to pass the dough through the sheeter in this way until you have passed it through the gauge.

i) Place the sheeted dough on the prepared baking sheet and repeat, sheeting the remaining segments in the same way and dusting the sheeted pasta with semolina to prevent the sheets from sticking together.

j) Use the shapes or place the baking sheet in the freezer for several hours until the pasta is frozen. Try to resist the temptation to freeze them for any longer than 2 weeks. The freezer will dehydrate the pasta, causing it to crack and break and lose its toothsome texture.

k) Salt the water and cook pasta al dente.

l) Drain the pasta quickly, leaving a little water still dripping from the pasta, then quickly add it to the pan with the sauce.

CONCLUSION

Pasta comes in many different forms, shapes and sizes. It's not simply a matter of creating the pasta dough. It's also what you intend to do with it once you have made it. For example, the easiest thing to do with pasta dough is to roll it and then cut into long Linguine type strips. This is pasta making at its most basic and is often the first choice for pasta newbies. However, there is a lot more that can be achieved and this book will show you what else you could do with your freshly made pasta dough.

www.ingramcontent.com/pod-product-compliance
Lightning Source LLC
Chambersburg PA
CBHW070647120526
44590CB00013BA/861